The
That

- about two Irishmen who walked **out** of a bar *(p. 110)*
- what has four legs and chases cats *(p. 7)*
- the difference between a bitch and a slut *(p. 69)*
- how to clear out an Iraqi bingo game *(p. 4)*
- the most popular man in a nudist colony *(p. 26)*
- the most popular woman in a nudist colony *(p. 26)*
- why Viagra is like Disney World *(p. 46)*
- the one about the Polish kidnappers *(p. 40)*

...and hundreds more jokes, riddles, stories, and one-liners

The New York City
Bartender's
Joke Book

THE NEW YORK CITY Bartender's JOKE BOOK

JIMMY PRITCHARD

WARNER BOOKS

An AOL Time Warner Company

WARNER BOOKS EDITION

Cover design by Jon Valk
Text illustrations by Cliff Mott
Book design and text composition by Ellen Gleeson

Warner Books, Inc.,
1271 Avenue of the Americas,
New York, NY 10020

Visit our Web site at
www.twbookmark.com.

For information on Time Warner Trade Publishing's online publishing program, visit www.ipublish.com.

An AOL Time Warner Company

Printed in the United States of America

First Printing: January 2002

10 9 8 7 6 5 4 3 2 1

To my Father and Mother,
Jim and Mimi Pritchard, who gave me sunshine
and good humor.

To my wife Lisa, who laughs with me and at me
and soothes life's shocks.

And
The late William McGlynn

Acknowledgments

I would like to thank Betsy Mitchell at Warner Books, who took the ball and handed off to Jaime Levine, who loves jokes and ran for a touchdown.

I would like to thank my sister Linda, who finally "gets" my jokes, my little sister Jennifer, who always laughs at my jokes and my brother Shawn, who always tries to "one-up" me. Thanks kids!

Total thanks to my sons: Matthew, who has my knack for telling stories, and Michael, who has a knack for shortening the stories!

Thanks to Michael C. Hutchinson, who always, without fail, makes me laugh, Harry and Betsy Stout, Tim and Kathleen Remy, Frank and Jane Tourigney, Gregg and Shelly Garner, Larry Aschenbrenner, Eric Aschenbrenner, Joe Safron, Erinn and Kevin Gibbons, Stephanie Pritchard and Takako Pritchard, without all of whom I wouldn't have anyone to try out my jokes on.

Thanks to the jokesters, who keep me on my toes: Jon Aimone, Jim "The Big One" Barry, Alan Browdy, Dan "Bull" Bullington, Dave Cohen, Anthony Collins, The Doyle, Eric Floyd, Jack Foley,

Don Gehan, Greg Getz, Cary Gilbert, Johnny Girouard, Tim Grant, Pete Hendrixson, Pete Iulo, Rob Kuhar, Dave Leonard, John McKerrow, Joe McWilliams, Alan Mervish, "Saturday Night" Dave Muhlfelder, Dave Perrine, Kevin "Duffy" Philzone, Dave Ranghelli, Peter Stark, Michael Saposnic, and Soupy Sales.

Also thanks to: Cliff Mott, Kitty Kelly, OTB Annie, Hal Baum, Andy Ganzi, Jill Gaspar, Kevin O'Keefe, Kevin Gallagan, Keith Arrington, Kenny Taylor, Ron Fowler, Jack Roberts, Brad Gansberg, Luke Ratray, Paul Hovis and Deb Rascoe Hovis, Genji Ridley, John Earl Stevens, Mark Thalmayr, Steve Love, Todd "Little Todd" Engle, Tom "Two Shoes" Schmid, Dave Fogelman, Craig Magee, George Egan, John Littlefield, Jay Bayala, Kent Bearden, Bill and Anna Simmons, Christine Chagnon, Tom and Carol Constantin, Roxanne Ricker, Dave Nichols, Kelly Melson, Tim and Flo Stella, Kurt Coble, Nadine Link, "Stagehand" Scott, Bill at N.B.C., Sam from Houston, Jane from Charlotte, N.C., Kathleen, Frank from England, John from Lake Placid, Ron from England, Jim and Gloria from Scotland, Larry from Seattle, Joe from Croton, N.Y., Ronny McWilliams at Victory Café, Carol-Anne at Rathbone's Pub, Hugh at O'Lunney's Pub, Jimmy Glenn at Jimmy's Corner, Danno at Matt's Grill, Carmine's in the theater district and on the upper west side, Michael Ronis at Virgil's Real BBQ, and to everyone who told me a joke!

Thank you all!

What's the difference between God
and a bartender?
God never wanted to be a bartender.

ANTHONY, A BARTENDER

Introduction

Bob Hope once said that there are only four jokes, but I don't know what they are. I do know that every joke ends up being someone's misfortune, but we laugh anyway. The proverbial banana peel.

The dictionary says that a joke is an amusing story, especially one with a punch line. Someone is usually a punch line. Someone's misfortune. Someone always gets it in the end. One man's adversity is another man's joke. And we laugh.

How old are jokes, anyway? Well, since time began, probably. Adam might have had a joke or two, then Eve came along and she certainly had some jokes for, or about, Adam. Maybe that's where all the "size" jokes started.

Since I can remember, there have been "God" jokes, "God and Moses" jokes, "Jesus" jokes, "Jesus and Moses" jokes, and so on. Were Jesus and his disciples telling jokes at the Last Supper? "Hey Jesus, did you hear the one about . . . ." says Paul.

Were the Egyptians telling jokes as they wrapped King Tut? The Jews had to be telling jokes as they wandered around the desert for forty years. What else did they have to talk about? "Hey Irving, did you see that interesting rock about five miles back?"

The first recollection of humor, I suppose, was during medieval times. The court jester. He was there to entertain, to make the king laugh, probably to save his own neck.

And all this evolved to burlesque, to Vaudeville, to Bob Hope et al. —and those four jokes.

I found out at a young age that jokes were the "great equalizer." I've avoided a lot of fights by telling jokes. I felt like the court jester, saving my own neck and my nose.

One summer a few years ago, as I was wandering around the desert called Connecticut, on my way to Massachusetts, the Promised Land (because my parents promised me I could swim in their pool!), I had an idea. How many jokes do I know? As I lounged around the pool, steno pad and pen in hand, with Mom waiting on me hand and foot and Dad wondering when I was going back to New York, I wrote down, off the top of my head, mostly punch lines, close to a hundred jokes. That's when I started "collecting." I would ask anyone I met for a joke, usually getting "I heard a great one yesterday but I can't remember it" in reply. So, instead of asking for jokes, I would tell a few, like I always do anyway, and that usually started the ball rolling A joke begets a joke begets a joke.

Now I have a major collection for you to enjoy. Thrill your neighbors, impress your friends, and remember the lecture-circuit credo: "Always open with a joke."

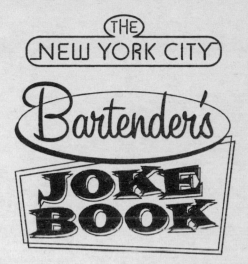

THE
NEW YORK CITY
Bartender's
JOKE BOOK

An old man walks into a bar, sits down, and starts crying. The bartender asks, "What's wrong?"

The old man looks at the bartender through teary eyes and between sobs says, "I married a beautiful woman two days ago. She's a natural blonde, twenty-five, intelligent, a marvelous cook, a meticulous housekeeper, extremely sensitive to my wants and needs, very giving, my best friend, and intensely passionate in bed."

The bartender stares at the old man for a brief moment and says, "But that sounds great! You have what every man wants in a woman, so why are you crying?"

The old man looks at the bartender and says, "*I can't remember where I live!*"

What's the best thing about having Alzheimer's disease?
You get to hide your own Easter eggs.

Two Irish guys are in a New York City bar. They are the only customers. The first Irish guy asks the second Irish guy, "How long have you been in the city?"

The second Irish guy says, "One year."

The first guy says, "One year?! I've been in the city for a year as well. Let's toast to being in the city for a year!" They both down a shot of Irish whiskey.

The first guy asks, "What part of Ireland are you from?"

The second guy says, "I'm from County Cork."

The first guy says, "I'm from County Cork as well! Let's drink to Cork!" They both down another shot.

The first guy asks, "What town in Cork are you from?"

The second guy says, "I grew up in the town of Kinsale."

"Jesus, Mary, and Joseph!!" the first guy exclaims. "I grew up in Kinsale as well! Let's drink to Kinsale!" They both down another shot.

The first guy asks, "On what street did you live?"

The second guy says, "I lived on Carney Street."

"I can't fuckin' believe it!" the first guy says. "I lived on Carney Street as well! Let's drink to Carney Street!" They both down yet another shot.

All of a sudden the telephone rings and the bartender answers it. "Oh, hello, Boss. No, it's pretty quiet, except the O'Brian twins are here, drunk again."

An old man and an old woman have been married for over fifty years. Their children are grown and spread out across the country with families of their own. The old man and old woman are sitting in rocking chairs on their porch watching the sunset as they have done for the past twenty-five years.

All of a sudden, the old woman stands up and backhands the old man. He falls off the rocking chair, gets up, straightens his hair, puts his glasses back on and asks, "What the hell was that for?"

The old woman looks at him and says, "That's for fifty years of lousy sex!"

The old man says, "Oh," and sits back down in his rocker.

Less than a minute later the old man stands up and backhands the old woman. She falls out of her rocker, rolls across the porch, and stops at the railing. She gets up, pulls her dress down, makes sure her teeth are secure and asks, "What the hell was that for?"

The old man points his finger at her and says, "That's for knowing the difference!"

Why don't women fart as much as men?
They can't keep their mouths shut long enough to build up the pressure.

After a few drinks a man wanders out of a pub in Belfast and walks up a deserted alley. All of a sudden a man with a gun steps out of a doorway and asks him, "Are you Catholic or Protestant?"

The man thinks to himself, "If I tell him I'm Catholic and he's Protestant, I'm a dead man. But if I say I'm Protestant and he's Catholic, he'll shoot me for sure." So he quickly says, "I'm Jewish!"

The man with the gun says, "Well, I must be the luckiest Palestinian in all of Ireland!"

How do you clear out an Iraqi bingo game?
Yell "B-52!"

An old woman is wheeling around the nursing home in her wheelchair. She rolls up to an old man sitting in his own wheelchair, taps him on his arm, and says, "I bet I can guess how old you are."

"No you can't," the old man responds.

"I bet I can guess how old you are."

"No you can't, leave me alone."

"I bet I can guess how old you are."

"No you can't, go away."

"I bet I can guess how old you are."

"*All right, all right!*" the old man says, exasperated. "Go ahead, guess how old I am!"

She reaches over and unzips his fly, puts her hand in his pants and jiggles his balls around for a minute, then takes her hand out and says, "You're eighty-seven years old."

"That's right!" the old man says, astounded. "That's amazing! How did you do that?"

With a wry smile, the old woman says, "You told me yesterday."

A sex therapist has a theory. He is convinced that people who have sex one or more times a day are the happiest people on the planet. He randomly selects 1,500 people and invites them to a seminar at the local town hall. There, the therapist walks up to the podium and says, "With a show of hands, how many of you have sex one or more times a day?"

A little more than half of the people quickly raise their hands, and every one of them has a huge grin on their face or they are laughing hysterically.

The therapist smiles, knowing that his theory is holding true. "Now," he says, "how many of you have sex only once a week?"

A little less than half raise their hands, a thin grin on their faces.

Again the therapist smiles, knowing that his theory is still holding true. Then he says, "How many of you have sex once a month?"

Only a few people lift their hands, and as if they are embarrassed there are no smiles on any of their faces.

The therapist is pleased, knowing that his theory will soon be fact. "I have one more question," he states. "How many of you have sex only once a year?"

Everyone looks around, noting that no hands are raised, but way in the back of the hall one man is jumping up and down, frantically raising his hand, laughing uncontrollably.

The therapist is shocked. One man has single-handedly disproved his theory!

"Sir," he exclaims, "you only have sex once a year; why are you so happy?"

The man, hardly able to contain himself, yells, "*Today's the day*!"

What has four legs and chases cats?
Mrs. Katz and her attorney.

Υ

A priest and a construction worker are flying from New York to California. The priest is sitting at the window seat diligently toiling away at the *New York Times* crossword puzzle while the construction worker is snoozing on the aisle seat. After a while, the priest gently nudges the construction worker, hoping to wake him. The construction worker opens his eyes and says, "Yes, Father, what can I do for you?"

"I wonder if you could help me with this crossword puzzle?" the priest answers, somewhat apologetically.

"Sure, Father," the construction worker says eagerly. "I'd be glad to."

"Well," says the priest sheepishly, "I need a four-letter word that ends in U-N-T that means 'female relative.'"

"That's easy, Father," says the construction worker. "The word you are looking for is A-U-N-T."

"Oh! That's right!" the priest says triumphantly. "Do you have an eraser?"

Υ

When I fly anywhere, I sleep like a baby. I throw up and poop in my pants!

Two old ladies are on vacation in Scotland. They visit various little towns, buying souvenirs and meeting the lovely country folk. One day, driving their rented car out in the country, they come upon a scene one would only see in photographs—a beautiful field with one solitary, majestic oak tree with a white stone wall behind it and a Scotsman, wearing the traditional kilt, sleeping at the base of the tree.

The ladies get out of the car to take some pictures. One old lady whispers to the other, "I wonder if what they say is true, that Scotsmen don't wear anything under their kilts."

"Let's find out," responds the other lady with a wink and a grin.

The two ladies then tiptoe up to the Scotsman

by the tree and gently lift up his kilt. Lo and behold, he doesn't have any underpants on! But he must have been having one helluva dream, if you get my drift.

One old lady opens her purse and extracts a blue ribbon and ties it in a bow around the Scotsman's penis. They giggle, take a picture, pull his kilt down ever so gently, go back to the car, and drive off.

Half an hour later, the Scotsman wakes up and stretches. He has to pee, so he pulls up his kilt, looks down, sees the ribbon, and exclaims, "Well, I dinna know where ya bin when I was sleepin' but I'm proud o' ya . . . ya won first prize!"

🍸

What is Irish foreplay?
"Brace yourself, Erin, here I come!"

🍺

What is 5 miles long, has 140,000 pairs of legs, and an IQ of 150?
The St. Patrick's Day Parade.

🍸

Did you know that Ted Kennedy spent five million dollars on his last campaign?
He got most of it back when he returned the empties.

And speaking of kilts ...

It was the summer between the end of high school and the beginning of college. I had the opportunity to visit Scotland, hitchhiking transversely, north to south, east to west, wide-eyed and enthralled at the beauty of the Highlands.

Not far from Edinburgh is the lovely town of Haddington, where I met the McTavish clan. They took me in as if I were one of their own and invited me to their annual party, usually reserved for family and friends—no outsiders.

It was at this party that I had the privilege and honor to wear, for the entire evening, the traditional kilt, with the socks, the shoes, the blouse, and the pouch. I danced some Scottish jigs, sang some Scottish songs, and drank some scotch whiskey. Then I met Maggie! Red of hair and green of eyes, a beauty that would stop *all* wars!

As if drawn by a huge magnet, we found ourselves outside walking along the glen; the mist was rising, the moon was full, and the sound of the bagpipes could be heard off in the distance.

After a short while, she stopped and looked at me with those beautiful green eyes and said, "You'd like to hold my hand, wouldn't ya?"

I smiled and said, "Yes, Maggie, I'd love to hold your hand. How could you tell?"

"From the twinkle in your eyes," she said, smiling.

So we walked along the glen, holding hands— the mist rising, the moon full, and the bagpipes droning in the distance. She stopped me again, looked at me with those beautiful green eyes and said, "You'd like to put your arm around me, now wouldn't ya?"

"Yes, Maggie," I said, "I'd love to put my arm around you. How could you tell?"

"From the twinkle in your eyes," she said.

So we walked along the glen, arms around each other; the mist was rising, the moon was full, and the bagpipes were droning in the distance. She stopped and looked at me with her beautiful green eyes and said, "You'd like to kiss me, wouldn't ya?"

"Oh yes, Maggie," I said, "I'd love to kiss you. How could you tell?"

"From the twinkle in your eyes," she said.

And we kissed! We kissed long and we kissed deep and we kissed passionately. And of all the kisses throughout history, it had to be *the number one kiss of all time*!

As the mist rose, the moon shone, and the bagpipes droned in the distance, she pulled away slightly and looked at me with those beautiful green eyes and said, "You'd like to bed me down now, wouldn't ya?"

"Oh yes, Maggie I'd love to bed you down! You could tell that from the twinkle in my eyes?"

With a twinkle in her own eyes she said, "No, from the tilt in yer kilt!"

Why do Canadians like to have sex doggy style?
So they both can watch the hockey game.

Did you hear about the guy who divorced his wife because she wouldn't do it doggy style?
She refused to go out on the front lawn.

God wants to go on vacation, but he's not sure where to go, so he asks St. Peter for some suggestions. St. Peter says, "Mercury. Why don't you go to Mercury for your vacation?"

"No," answers God. "I'm not going to Mercury. I was there two million years ago and I got the worst sunburn ever. I couldn't move for a week, no amount of lotions or creams helped. No, it's too hot there and I'll never go back."

"Pluto," responds St. Peter, eager to please. "Why don't you go to Pluto?"

"Forget it!" retorts God. "I went to Pluto one million years ago and got frostbitten so bad I almost lost my toes! No, it's too cold there, I'll never go back."

"I've got it!" St. Peter exclaims. "Earth, why don't you go to Earth for your vacation?"

"What are you, nuts?" God fumes. "I was there two thousand years ago and they're still giving me shit for knocking up that Jewish chick!"

Did you hear about the four-passenger airplane
that crashed in a Polish cemetery?
*So far they have recovered three
hundred bodies.*

Υ

An old guy walks into St. Patrick's Cathedral
and stands in line for confession. Finally it is his
turn and he enters the confessional and sits down.
The priest asks, "How can I help you, my son?"

The guy says, "I just had sex with two beautiful
eighteen-year-old twin girls!"

"When was the last time you were in church to
confess your sins?" asked the priest.

"Well," says the guy, "I've never been to church.
In fact, I'm Jewish."

"Then why are you telling me this?" asks the
priest.

"Are you kidding me?" yells the guy. "I'm telling
everybody!"

Three dogs, two mutts and a German shepherd, are at the ASPCA. The first mutt asks the second mutt, "What are you doing here?"

"Well," replies the second mutt, "I got a little antsy one day, so I dug a hole under the fence and ran around the neighborhood. It was a beautiful day and I was having fun when I caught a scent in the air, so I followed it. I ended up in the backyard of a beautiful collie, a breeding collie, with papers no less. I couldn't resist it, so I jumped over the fence and mounted her. A few months later she has puppies, her owner says something to my owner, and he brings me here to have my nuts cut."

"Oh," says the first mutt.

The second mutt asks the first mutt, "What are you doing here?"

The first mutt says, "Well, I'm a horny kind of dog. My master comes home, I hump his leg. His wife comes home, I hump her leg. The children come home, I'm humping their legs. Tables, chairs, anything with legs, I'm humping it. So my owner brought me here to get my nuts cut."

"Oh," says the second mutt.

They both look at the German shepherd and in unison ask, "What are *you* doing here?"

The German shepherd says, "Well, my owner is a tall, unbelievably gorgeous blonde. She's taking a shower one day and I happen to be in the bathroom. She steps out of the shower, dripping wet. She bends over to pick up the towel, and I see a sight that I cannot resist! So I mount her!"

"Oh, so you're here to get your nuts cut too," says one of the mutts.

"Hell, no!" snorts the German shepherd. "I'm here for a manicure!"

Why do dogs lick their balls?
Because they can.
or
Because they want to.
or
Because no one else will.
or
Because they can't make a fist.
or
To get the taste of mailmen out of their mouth.

How do you stop a dog from humping your leg?
Suck his dick.

Two golfers are on the sixteenth tee when, out of the clear blue, they are both hit by the same lightning bolt and die. They arrive in heaven and are greeted by St. Peter, who looks through the Big Admittance Book and sees that no golfers are due on that day and realizes that there has been a mistake.

"Look," St. Peter says apologetically, "there has been a terrible mistake. You weren't supposed to die yet, and to make it up to you, I'm authorized to send you back to Earth as anything you want."

One golfer jumps at the chance and says, "I want to go back as a lesbian!"

The other golfer says, "What the hell do you want to go back as a lesbian for?"

The golfer smiles and says, "Because, my friend, I'll get all the pussy I want and I can hit from the red tees!"

Two lesbian frogs are having sex when one says to the other, "Hey, they're right, we *do* taste like chicken!"

A boy asks his father for help with his homework. Being a good father, he turns off the television, puts his newspaper down and says, "Sure, Son, how can I help you?"

The boy says, "I'm having a hard time finding

the difference between 'theoretically' and 'realistically.'"

The father thinks for a minute and then says, "Son, I want you to go to your mother's room and ask her if she will have sex with any man for one million dollars."

The boy goes to his mother's room. He returns two minutes later and says, "Yeah, Mom says she will have sex with any man for one million dollars."

The father then says, "Now, I want you to go to your sister's room and ask her the same question."

The boy goes to his sister's room. He returns two minutes later and says, "Yeah, Sister says she will have sex with any man for one million dollars, too."

The father says, "Son, 'theoretically,' we are millionaires. 'Realistically,' we are living with a couple of whores!"

Yeah, right, just reverse it and ask any man if he'll sleep with any woman for one million dollars and ninety-nine percent of the male population will say, "Hell, I'll sleep with any woman for free!" The other one percent are dead.

What does a blonde say after multiple orgasms?
"Are, like, all you guys on the same team?"

A duck walks into the local pharmacy, waddles up to the counter, and says, "Hey, I need a condom!"

The pharmacist says, "Sure, do you want me to put it on your bill?"

The duck says, "What do you think I am, a weirdo?!"

What do you call a dog with no legs?
*Nothing—he can't come when you call
him anyway.*

A duck walks into a bar, walks up to the bartender, and says, "Hey, you got any duck food?"

The bartender looks at the duck and says, "No, I don't got any duck food. Now get outta here, beat it."

The next day, the duck walks back into the same bar and says, "Hey, you got any duck food?"

The bartender says, "Look, I told you yesterday, I don't have any duck food! Get outta here, beat it, scram, and don't come back!"

The next day the duck walks back into the same bar and says, "Hey, you got any duck food?"

The bartender says, "Listen, if you come back here one more time, I'm going to get a handful of nails and I'm going to nail your web feet right to the floor where you're standing! I don't have any duck food, never did have any duck food, and I'm not going to get any duck food, ever! Now beat it, scram, get outta here, and don't ever come back!"

The next week the duck walks back into the same bar and says to the bartender, "Hey, you got any nails?"

"No," says the bartender, "I don't got any nails."

The duck says, "You got any duck food?"

How do you say hello to a duck?
"Hello, duck!"

Two nuns are riding their bicycles around the Vatican. After a while, one nun says, "Hey, I never came this way before."

The other nun says, "Yeah, I know. It's the cobblestones!"

Three nuns are sitting on a bench in Central Park, New York City. All of a sudden, a man wearing a trench coat flashes all three of them!

The first nun had a stroke! The second nun had a stroke!

The third nun couldn't reach!

A guy walks into a bar, sits down, and orders a martini. He downs the martini, opens his suit coat, and looks in the pocket. He orders another martini, finishes it, and looks in his pocket again. He orders another, downs it, and looks in his pocket a third time.

The bartender has been watching the guy and his curiosity gets the best of him. He asks, "Why do you keep looking in your pocket after each drink?"

The guy says, "I have a picture of my wife, and when she looks good I go home."

How are martinis like a woman's breasts?
One is not enough and three are too many.

An old man walks into a pizza parlor and tells the kid behind the counter, "I'd like a prune pizza."

The kid says, "What?"

"Prunes," the old man says. "Do you have any prunes?"

The kid says, "Yeah, we have prunes."

"Then," says the old man, "give me a prune pizza!"

The kid says, "Do you want that to go?"

The old man scowls and says, "Why else would I want it?!"

Did you hear about the guy who took Viagra,
but it got stuck in his throat?
He had a stiff neck all night.

A middle-aged couple get married and are in
the honeymoon suite when the bride takes off her
clothes and says to her new husband, "Honey, I
have to warn you. I have acute angina."

The husband looks at her and says, "Your tits
aren't bad either!"

What's the difference between ignorance
and indifference?
I don't know and I don't care!

A drunk tries to enter a bar, but the doorman
stops him and says, very politely, "I'm sorry, sir, but
you can't come in without a tie."

He staggers back to his car and fumbles
through the glove compartment. He finds thread,
string, and duct tape. No tie. So he lurches back to
the trunk of the car and pulls out the jumper
cables. He puts the cables around his neck and ties
a nice Windsor knot. He walks back to the bar and
right up to the doorman.

The doorman looks at him and the jumper cables around his neck and says, "All right, you can come in, but don't start anything!"

What's the difference between a drunk and an alcoholic?
We don't have to go to those dopey meetings!

A drunk walks into a bar. He receives five stitches.

Mrs. O'Reilly comes home from the doctor's office and tells her husband, "Paddy, the doctor says that I'm pregnant."

Paddy says, "That can't be! We've been very careful!"

She says, "I know, Paddy, but to be sure, he wants me to come back tomorrow with a sample."

"Well," says Paddy, "what's a sample?"

"I don't know what a sample is," she says. "I didn't want the doctor to think I was dumb, so I didn't ask him."

Paddy says, "Go ask Mrs. O'Brian what a sample is, she has twelve kids, she might know."

So Mrs. O'Reilly goes down the street to Mrs. O'Brian's house. A half hour later she comes back with a black eye, missing teeth, and her clothes torn and ripped. Paddy sees her and says, "What the hell happened?"

"Well, Paddy," she says. "I went to Mrs. O'Brian's house like you said and I asked her what a sample was and she told me to piss in a cup and I told her to shit in her handbag and the fight was on!"

🍸

Three debutantes are in a car driving around in the South. They pass a beautiful horse farm with beautiful green pastures, beautiful white fences, and beautiful white stables with beautiful horses. The debutante in the backseat says, "My daddy bought me this beautiful horse farm for graduating high school!"

The debutante in the passenger seat says, "Oooooooh!"

The debutante that's driving says, "That's nice."

After a while, they pass a beautiful golf course, hotel, and casino. The debutante in the passenger seat says, "My daddy bought me this beautiful golf course, hotel, and casino for graduating high school!"

The debutante in the backseat says, "Oooooooh!"

The debutante that's driving says, "That's nice."

The debutante in the backseat asks the debutante that's driving, "What did your daddy buy you for graduating high school?"

The debutante that's driving says, "My daddy is of limited means and all he gave me was advice."

The debutante in the front seat asks the debutante driving, "What was the advice your daddy gave you for graduating high school?"

The debutante that's driving says, "My daddy always told me to say 'That's nice' instead of saying 'Go fuck yourself!'"

What's the difference between a blonde and a mosquito?
A mosquito stops sucking after you slap it.

Two guys are walking their dogs. One guy sees a bar across the street and says to the other guy, "What do you say we go in that bar for a cold beer?"

The other guy says, "Forget it! They will never let us in with our dogs."

"Listen," says the first guy. "Watch what I do and repeat what I say and I guarantee that we will be in that bar, with our dogs, drinking an ice-cold beer."

He puts his sunglasses on, takes his dog by the leash, and walks across the street. Just as he gets to the bar, the doorman says, "Sorry, no dogs allowed."

"Oh, this is my seeing-eye dog," says the guy.

Very apologetically, the doorman opens the door and lets the guy in with his dog.

The guy across the street smiles, puts his sunglasses on, takes his dog by the leash, and walks to the bar. The doorman stops him and says, "Sorry, no dogs allowed."

The guy says, "This is my seeing-eye dog."

The doorman looks at the dog and says, "Since when do they have Chihuahuas as seeing-eye dogs?"

Not missing a beat, the guy says, "*They gave me a Chihuahua*?!"

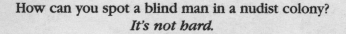

How can you spot a blind man in a nudist colony?
It's not hard.

Who is the most popular man in a nudist colony?
The one who can carry two cups of coffee and twelve doughnuts.

Who is the most popular woman in a nudist colony?
The one who can eat the twelve doughnuts.

What has four legs and an arm?
A Doberman pinscher.

Hear about the new Korean cookbook?
It's called One Hundred Ways
to Wok Your Dog.

What's the difference between beer nuts
and deer nuts?
Deer nuts are always under a buck.

What is a Polish ménage à trois?
Two of the people watch.

*O.K., this one is for all you Baby Boomers out
there. Remember the TV series Gunsmoke?*

It's a hot day in Dodge City. So hot that no one
is out on the street. But Marshal Dillon is on the
porch of the jailhouse anyway, sitting in a chair
watching the street like a good marshal.

Out of the corner of his eye, Dillon sees someone walking up the street at the edge of town. He
stands up to get a better look and sees that it is
Festus with hat, boots, and a gun belt, but other-
wise totally naked.

Dillon runs into the jailhouse, grabs a blanket,
and runs down the street to Festus and wraps the

blanket around him. "Dang gum it, Festus, what the hell are you doing?" he asks.

"Well, Marshal Dillon," says Festus, "I was sweeping the porch of the jailhouse like you told me, when Miss Kitty came riding up on her buggy and she says to me, 'Festus, it is real hot out here, would you like to come up to the plateau, where it's nice and cool, with me?'

"Well, Marshal," continues Festus, "you know how I feel about Miss Kitty, so I got up on the buggy, took the reins, and headed off to the plateau with her.

"Once we got to the plateau, Miss Kitty says to me, 'Festus, I have a picnic basket that is just too heavy for me to lift, could you get it off the buggy for me?'

"Well, Marshal, you know how I feel about Miss Kitty, so I took the picnic basket off the buggy and put it on the ground. Then Miss Kitty says to me, 'Festus, there is a blanket on the buggy, could you get it and spread it on the ground for me?'

"Well, Marshal, you know how I feel about Miss Kitty, so I took the blanket and spread it out on the ground the way she wanted. Then she says to me, 'Festus, I have too much food in this picnic basket for one person. Would you like to join me in a picnic?'

"Well, Marshal Dillon, you know how I feel about Miss Kitty, so we commenced to eatin' home-made fried chicken and homemade potato salad up there on the plateau where it's nice and cool, and when we was done, Miss Kitty says to me, 'Festus, I want you to stand up, turn around, and take off all your clothes.'

"Wellll, Marshal Dillon, you *know* how I feel about Miss Kitty, so I turned around and took all my clothes off, and when I turned back, there was Miss Kitty, buck naked and spread-eagled on the picnic blanket, and she looked at me and said, 'Well, Festus, go to town!'

"So, Marshal Dillon, here I am!"

Why are cowgirls bowlegged?
Cowboys like to eat with their hats on.

John Wayne rides into town with the cavalry. He rides right up to the first house of ill repute he finds. He gets off his horse and knocks on the door.

The madam of the house opens the door and says, "How can I help you?"

John Wayne says, "Well, how much would you charge for my company?"

"Ooooh," says the madam, looking John Wayne up and down with a big grin. "Ten dollars," she says.

John Wayne turns, raises his arm, and yells, "*Company hooooo!*"

Roy Rogers is down by the creek fishing when the cavalry rides up. The sergeant of the cavalry says, "Roy,

Roy, the Indians burned down your ranch!"

Roy throws down his fishing pole angrily and starts running toward the ranch.

"Wait, Roy," says the sergeant. "Come back, there's more!" Roy comes back and the sergeant says, "They raped Dale!"

Infuriated, Roy turns and starts running toward the ranch.

"Wait, Roy, come back, there's more," the sergeant says. Roy comes back and the sergeant says, "They stole Trigger too!"

Now Roy is really pissed off, and he heads toward the ranch.

The sergeant says, "Roy, wait!"

Roy Rogers comes back and with hatred in his eyes yells, "What!"

The sergeant says, "How 'bout a song before you go?"

The Lone Ranger and Tonto are riding along the prairie, making sure the land is safe from the bad guys. They stop for a moment and Tonto gets down off his horse, puts his ear to the ground, and says, "Buffalo come."

The Lone Ranger, still on his horse, looks around the prairie and says, "Tonto, how can you tell?"

Tonto replies, "Ear sticky."

After patrolling the plains, the Lone Ranger and Tonto gallop back to town. They stop in front of the first saloon they come to and get off their horses.

"Tonto," says the Lone Ranger, "the horses are hot. I want you to run around the horses as fast as you can. The wind from your running will cool them off. I'll be in the saloon having a drink."

Being ever so faithful, Tonto runs around the horses.

After a half hour, a guy steps into the saloon and says, "Hey, who owns the white stallion out front?"

The Lone Ranger says, "I do, why?"

The guy says, "You left your Injun running!"

A Native American is accepted to M.I.T. and after four long years of hard work he graduates with honors, top of his class.

He goes back to the reservation and says to his father, "Father, for years you have sacrificed everything to send me to an expensive American school. Now I am back and I would like to repay you for all that you have done. Please, Father, is there anything I can do for you?"

His father, being very old, says, "Help me up." The son helps his father up. The father says, "Come."

They walk very slowly to the outhouse, fifty yards away. When they reach the outhouse, the father says, "I am old and cannot see very well. Put light in outhouse."

"Father," says the son, "after all the schooling and all the knowledge I have learned, I can move you out of the reservation and you can live in comfort and luxury for the remainder of your life and all you want me to do is put a light in the outhouse?"

"Yes," says the father, "that is all I want. That is all I need. Put light in outhouse."

So the son builds a generator, runs a line to the

outhouse, hooks up a socket, and screws in a light-bulb.

And so the son becomes the first Native American to wire a head for a reservation.

Υ

A guy runs into a psychiatrist's office and says, "Doc, I'm a teepee, I'm a wigwam, I'm a teepee, I'm a wigwam, I'm a teepee, I'm a wigwam!"

The psychiatrist says, "Relax, you're two tents!"

A young, naive Native American girl wonders why the men wear feathers. She sees a young brave with one feather and asks what the feather means.

"One feather, one squaw," says the brave.

She walks along and sees another brave with two feathers and asks what they mean.

"Two feathers, two squaws," says the brave.

After a while, she sees the chief with a full headdress of feathers, from the top of his head all the way to the ground. "Chief, what do all those feathers mean?" she asks.

"I have many squaws," the chief says, "Squaws in the mountains, squaws across the great sea, squaws in the plains and desert."

"Oh, dear!" exclaims the girl.

"No," says the chief, "ass too high, run too fast!"

Υ

Why were Native Americans the first ones
in this country?
They had reservations.

A prospector has been up in the mountains panning for gold for two years when he finally finds a small amount of gold dust. He puts the gold dust into a pouch, cleans himself up a little, and heads into town.

He stops at the nearest saloon—which is the only saloon in town—walks up to the bar, dumps the gold dust on the bar, points to it, and says, "Bartender, I want to get likkered up and I want me a woman!"

The bartender says, "Well, I can get you all the liquor you want, but I can't get you no woman, they all left town a couple of years ago. But we do have Injun Joe behind that door."

"Oh, no, no," says the prospector, "I don't go in for that kind of stuff!" So he drinks till the gold dust is gone and staggers back up the mountain.

Another two years go by before the prospector finds a couple of gold nuggets. He puts them in his pouch, cleans up a bit, and heads for town.

He stops at the nearest saloon—the only saloon in town—walks up to the bar, dumps the gold nuggets on the bar, points to the gold nuggets, and says to the bartender, "Bartender, I want to get likkered up and I want me a woman!"

The bartender says, "Well, I can get you good and likkered up, but we haven't had any women here for a few years, but we do have Injun Joe behind that door."

"Oh, no, no!" says the prospector, "I don't go in for that kind of stuff!" So he drinks until the gold nuggets are gone and staggers back up the mountain.

One more year goes by and the prospector hits it big! Four huge gold nuggets! He shoves the nuggets into his pockets, doesn't bother to clean himself up, and heads for town.

He stops at the nearest saloon—which is still the only saloon in town—runs up to the bar, slams the gold nuggets on the bar, and yells, "Bartender! I want to get likkered up!" He grabs the bartender by the tie. "*And I need a woman!*"

The bartender says, "Well, I sure can get you all the liquor you want, but there ain't no women in town, they left a while back, but we do have Injun Joe behind that door."

"Oh, no, no," says the prospector, "I don't go in for that kind of stuff." But as he drinks, he starts to get a little randy. He calls the bartender over and says, "Bartender, how much do you charge for that Injun Joe behind that door?"

The bartender says, "Fifty dollars."

"Fifty dollars!?" says the prospector. "How do you justify fifty dollars?"

"Well," says the bartender, "we give Injun Joe ten dollars, and twenty dollars apiece for two guys to hold him down, 'cause Injun Joe don't go in for that kind of stuff either."

A guy is riding his snowmobile in Alaska. He's out on the tundra, twenty-five to thirty miles from the nearest town, when all of a sudden the snowmobile stops running. He can't get it started and panic sets in because the sun is setting and he'll freeze to death if he is stranded there overnight.

Then, to his amazement, he sees an Eskimo riding a snowmobile along the horizon, so he starts jumping up and down, waving his arms, hoping to get the Eskimo's attention.

The Eskimo sees him and heads toward him. Fifteen minutes later, the Eskimo pulls up next to him and asks, "What's the problem?"

The guy says, "I don't know. I'm riding along when all of a sudden it stops and I can't get it started."

"Well," says the Eskimo, "I'm an expert snowmobile mechanic, let me take a look at it." He opens the engine cover, looks at the engine, goes back to his snowmobile, gets some tools, and starts tinkering with the motor. After a couple of minutes, he says, "I found the problem."

The guy asks, "What is it?"

The Eskimo says, "You blew a seal."

"Oh, no," the guy says. "That's just snow on my lip!"

After picking up a few items at a pharmacy, a guy goes up to the counter with a can of shaving cream, razor blades, soap, and toothpaste. The woman at the counter rings up the items and asks the guy, "You're single, aren't you?"

"Why, yes," answers the guy. "How can you tell?"

"Because you're fucking ugly!" replies the woman.

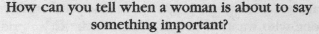

How can you tell when a woman is about to say something important?
She starts by saying, "A man once told me ..."

A young boy gets a train set for Christmas. His parents help him set it up and they all play with it. Eventually, the father goes into the den to catch up on

football scores and the mother goes into the kitchen to clean the Christmas dinner dishes. The boy is left alone in the living room playing with his train.

All of a sudden, the mom, in the kitchen, hears the boy, in the living room, say, "59th Street station, anyone who wants to get on, get the fuck on, anyone who wants to get off, get the fuck off!"

Not quite sure of what she heard, the mother stands next to the living-room door to listen. Much to her dismay, she hears her son say, "42nd Street, anyone who wants to get on, get the fuck on, anyone who wants to get off, get the fuck off!"

The mother rushes into the living room and grabs the boy by the neck and says, "I don't know where you learned that kind of language, certainly not from me and I hope not from your father. You are not to use that language *ever*!" With that, she drags the boy up the stairs and throws him in his room and says, "Now you stay in here until you have learned your lesson!"

She storms out and goes back downstairs to the kitchen, fuming. After an hour, she cools down and goes upstairs to the boy's room and says, "Have you learned your lesson?"

The boy says, "Yes, ma'am, I've learned my lesson, real good."

"All right," says the mother, "you can go back downstairs and play with your train set again."

Not quite sure if he learned his lesson or not, the mother stands near the living-room door to listen. She hears the boy say, "59th Street, anyone who wants to get on, get on, anyone who wants to get off, get off."

But just to be sure, the mother listens further, and she hears the boy say "42nd Street, anyone who wants to get on, get on, anyone who wants to get off, get off."

Satisfied that he has learned his lesson, she goes back into the kitchen to continue cleaning the Christmas dinner dishes.

There is a long pause. Silence from the living room. Then the mother hears the boy say, "14th Street, anyone who wants to get on, get on, anyone who wants to get off, get off.

"If anyone has any complaints about the delays in the system," the boy continues, "see the fucking bitch in the kitchen!"

🍸

Did you hear about the Energizer Battery bunny?
He died. Someone put the batteries in
backwards and he kept coming and coming
and coming …

🍺

It was comedy night at the Comic Strip, and this night featured a ventriloquist. Everything was going great, he had the audience in the palm of his hand, laughing, until he started with the Polish jokes—the ventriloquist and his dummy, back and forth with the Polish jokes, one after the other.

All of a sudden, a Polish guy stands up and yells, "Hey, I'm Polish, and we—yes, I'm speaking for all of us—we resent those jokes. As a matter of fact, they are not jokes to us! They are not funny. They are degrading, humiliating, and insulting! Please stop it!"

The ventriloquist is stunned. He has never encountered anything like this in his whole career. He stands up, still holding the dummy, and very apologetically says to the Polish guy, "I am very sorry, sir, to you and all the Polish people I have offended. From this moment on I will never, ever utter another Polish joke as long as I live, and I will urge my fellow comedians to follow suit. I apologize to you, sir, and anyone I have offended."

"Hey," says the Polish guy, "I'm not talking to you. I'm talking to the little guy!"

🍸

Did you hear about the Polish kidnappers?
They sent the kid home with the ransom note.
The parents must have been Polish too, because
they sent the kid back with the money.

🍺

An old woman is feeling poorly, so her husband takes her to the doctor for a checkup. The old man waits in the waiting room while the old lady and the doctor go into the examining room.

After a complete exam, the doctor brings the old woman into his office to ask her a few questions. "How are you sleeping?" he asks.

"I get eight hours of sleep," says the woman, "and sometimes I wake up to go to the bathroom, but I have no problem falling back asleep. Occasionally I take an afternoon nap for an hour, but all in all, I sleep just fine."

"How is your diet?" asks the doctor.

"I have three well-balanced meals a day," says the woman. "Sometimes I have a light snack between lunch and dinner, but I eat very well."

"Do you still have intercourse?" asks the doctor.

"What?" replies the woman.

"Intercourse," says the doctor. "Do you still have intercourse?"

The old woman gets up out of her chair and opens the door to the waiting room and asks her husband, "Honey, do we have intercourse?"

The old man looks at her and says, "If I've told you once I've told you a thousand times, it's Blue Cross Blue Shield!"

A husband and wife are driving down the interstate when they are pulled over by a state trooper. The trooper says to the husband, "I clocked you doing 90 mph in a 55 mph zone."

"That can't be," says the husband. "I always obey the speed limit."

"No you don't," says the wife. "You always speed no matter what the speed limit is!"

"Shut up, you bitch!" yells the husband to his wife.

The trooper says, "I see you are not wearing your seat belt."

"It must have slipped my mind," says the husband. "I always wear my seat belt."

"No you don't," says the wife. "You never put your seat belt on!"

"Shut up you bitch!" yells the husband to his wife.

"All right," says the trooper, "let me see your license and registration."

The husband fumbles through his pockets and says, "I must have left my license in my other jacket at home."

"You never carry your license," says the wife. "It's on your bureau in the bedroom!"

"Will you shut the fuck up, you fucking bitch!" yells the husband.

"Step out of the car, sir," says the trooper, and as the husband gets out to the car, the trooper leans in and asks the wife, "Does your husband always talk to you like that?"

"Oh, no," says the wife with a smile, "only when he's drunk!"

Do you know what the side effect of Viagra is?
Your wife's headaches come back.

Two sons want to do something different for their father's ninetieth birthday, so they hire a call girl. She shows up at the house and the sons tell her to go up the stairs to the bedroom where the father is.

She opens the bedroom door and sees the old man sitting on the side of his bed, and she says with enthusiasm, "I'm here to give you super sex!"

The old man looks at her and says, "I'll take the soup."

After a physical, a doctor tells an old man, "You have Alzheimer's disease."

The old man says, "What should I do?"

"Go home and forget about it," says the doctor.

How many men does it take to change
a roll of toilet paper?
No one knows. It's never been done.

Why do women wear makeup and perfume?
Because they're ugly and they smell bad.

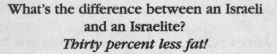

A Muslim dies and goes to heaven. He gets to the Pearly Gates and sees God standing there. He says to God, "I want to see Allah!"

"Allah is busy right now," says God.

"I want to see Allah *now*!" demands the Muslim.

God gets on the intercom and says, "Hey, Allah, when you're finished with the garbage, someone wants to see you!"

What's the difference between an Israeli and an Israelite?
Thirty percent less fat!

A guy is walking down the street when he passes a bar with a sign in the window that says, "1920 Prices." His curiosity gets the best of him and he goes inside.

The bartender says, "Hi, what can I get you?"

The guy asks, "How much is a beer?"

"Two cents," says the bartender.

"I'll have a beer," says the guy, smiling.

The bartender gives the guy a beer and the guy

gives the bartender a nickel and tells him to keep the change. Then he asks the bartender, "How much is a shot of whiskey?"

The bartender says, "Six cents."

The guy orders the whiskey, gives the bartender a dime, and tells him to keep the change.

As the guy is drinking his beer and sipping his whiskey, thinking about all the money he is saving, he notices two Hasidic Jews sitting at a table not drinking anything, just sitting there. He calls the bartender over and asks, "What's up with the two Jews?"

The bartender says, "Don't worry about them, they're just waiting for happy hour.

Why do all Hasidic Jews dress the same?
Only one of them is carrying the diamonds.

Do you know what the first Jewish settlement
in New York City was?
Ten cents on the dollar.

A boy asks his father, "Dad, can you get pregnant
from anal sex?"
*The father says, "How do you think
lawyers are born!"*

How is Viagra like Disney World?
There is an hour wait for a two-minute ride.

A husband comes home early from work. His wife is nowhere to be found, so he goes upstairs to the bedroom and sees her packing a suitcase. "What are you doing?" he asks.

"I'm going to Las Vegas," she says.

"Why are you going to Las Vegas?" he asks.

"I found out that I can get two hundred dollars for a blow job," she says.

The husband goes to the closet, pulls out his suitcase, and starts packing. "Where are you going?" asks the wife.

"I'm going to Las Vegas with you," replies the husband.

"What for?" asks the wife.

The husband says, "I want to see how long you can live on six hundred dollars a year."

What is every blonde's ambition in life?
To be like Vanna White and learn the alphabet.

In New Hampshire, the nor'easter is so strong, it completely destroys the widow Taylor's outhouse. The following spring, she hires Sam the carpenter to build her a new one. He works day and night and, finally, at week's end, the outhouse is finished. He tells her he'll come back in a few days to collect payment.

Three days later Sam the carpenter knocks on the widow Taylor's door. "Hello, widow Taylor, I'm here for payment for the outhouse."

"Nope, ain't goin' to pay ya," she says.

"Is anything wrong, widow Taylor?" asks Sam.

"Ain't goin' to pay ya," she replies.

Sam the carpenter figures that something is wrong with the outhouse, so he goes out back, with the widow Taylor following behind, to check it out. He looks at the outhouse—an all-pine frame, shingled roof, and a half-moon on the door. "I don't see anything wrong, widow Taylor," he says.

"Ain't goin' to pay ya," the widow Taylor says.

Shaking his head, Sam opens the door of the outhouse to look inside—all cedar, with two cushions on either side of the toilet, a magazine rack, and a nice reading lamp, plus a small cabinet to hold toilet paper and cleaning stuff. Sam asks, "Anything wrong in here, widow Taylor?"

"Ain't goin' to pay ya," she repeats.

Sam figures the only place left to look is in the toilet itself. He opens the lid of the toilet and sticks his head in to check it out.

Now, for those of you who don't know Sam the carpenter, he is a big, burly man with a completely bald head and a big bushy beard, and it is quite a sight to see him bent over with his head inside an outhouse toilet.

With his head in the toilet, Sam can't find anything wrong, but as he pulls his head out, one of the whiskers of his beard catches in a very small—invisible to the naked eye—crack in the seat, pulling the hair out. "*Owww*!" he yells.

The widow Taylor folds her arms, looks at Sam, and says, "Hurts, don't it?"

🍸

A man has a pit bull that is always biting everyone. After the latest incident, a cop suggests to the guy to get the dog's nuts cut and then he will be very docile and won't bite anyone. The man agrees and takes the dog to the veterinarian.

On the way, the dog gets loose and starts to attack a bum. The owner grabs the dog just as it is about to bite the bum. With his dog in control the guy says, "I'm sorry, I'm sorry, I'm on my way to the vet to get his nuts cut so he won't bite anyone anymore. I'm sorry!"

The bum looks at him and says, "Hell, don't cut his nuts off, pull out his teeth! I could see from a block away he wasn't going to fuck me!"

Where do you find a dog with no legs?
Right where you left him.

Why did the monkey fall out of the tree?
It was dead.

What has two legs, one wheel, and flies?
A wheelbarrow full of horse shit.

Two old ladies are in a bar talking. One old lady says, "My throat is sore. What do you take for a sore throat?"

"I suck on a Life Saver," says the other old lady.

"That's easy for you," says the first old lady. "You live at the beach!"

A sixty-year-old woman is lying in bed, reading, when she hears a voice say, "This is God. You have thirty-six more years to live and then you will come to heaven with me."

Early the next morning the lady goes to the beauty salon, where she gets her hair cut, colored, and styled. Then to a plastic surgeon to get a complete face-lift, including a nose job. After liposuction, breast augmentation, a manicure, and a pedicure, she goes to Bloomingdale's and buys a new wardrobe. She walks out of Bloomies looking like a million bucks.

Walking across the street, she gets hit by a bus and dies instantly. She goes to heaven, walks past St. Peter without saying a word, and marches right up to God, sticks her finger in his face and says angrily, "You said I had thirty-six more years to live!"

"I didn't recognize you!" says God.

A prostitute gets hit by a car. In the emergency room she tells the doctor that she thinks she's blind. The doctor asks, "How many fingers do I have up?"

"Oh my God," she cries. "I'm paralyzed too!"

An old guy goes into a bar and orders a bowl of soup. The bartender brings him the soup and walks away.

The old guy calls the bartender back and says, "Taste the soup."

"Is the soup too hot?" asks the bartender.

The old man shakes his head. "Taste the soup."

"Is it too cold?" asks the bartender.

"Taste the soup," says the old man.

"Is it too spicy?" asks the bartender, slightly annoyed.

"Taste the soup," repeats the old man.

"All right, all right," says the exasperated bartender. "Where's the spoon?"

"Ah-ha!" says the old man triumphantly.

A guy goes to a doctor's office with a carrot in one ear, a piece of celery in the other ear, and a mushroom stuck up his nose. The doctor takes one look at him and says, "You're not eating right!"

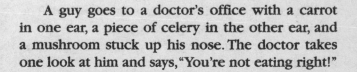

A ham sandwich walks into a bar. The bartender says, "Sorry, we don't serve food here."

A lady has two rabbits. She has had them since they were bunnies. They are housebroken. When she eats dinner, she puts their bowls of lettuce and carrots on the dining-room table and they all eat together. When she sleeps, she puts them on her bed and they all sleep together. She is very attached to the rabbits.

One day both rabbits die. The lady is heartbroken. She decides to have the rabbits stuffed so they will be with her for the rest of her life. She takes them to the taxidermist and tells him her story about the rabbits. The taxidermist sympathizes with the lady and says, "Don't worry, I'll do a real nice job for you, but let me ask you, would you like to have the rabbits mounted?"

"Oh no," says the lady. "Just holding hands will be nice."

Three ducks, in line, are crossing the road. The duck in the back says, "Quack, quack!"

The duck in front says, "Hey, I'm moving as fast as I can!"

If a sheep is a ram and a donkey is an ass, then why is a ram in the ass a goose?

🍸

A guy is walking around Chinatown, in New York City, and stops in a bar. "Give me a Stoli with a twist," he says to the bartender, who happens to be Chinese.

"A rong, rong, time ago, Cinderella was a man . . ." replies the bartender.

🍺

A manager of a warehouse hires a Chinese man to be in charge of supplies. He takes him to the supply room and tells him he will be back in two hours to check up on him.

After two hours, the manager goes to the supply room, only to find the door locked and the lights out. He unlocks the door and turns on the lights.

The Chinese man jumps up from behind a stack of boxes and yells, "SUPPLIES!"

A Greek restaurant owner always eats at the same Chinese restaurant and always orders fried rice just to hear the waiters say, "Flied lice," so he can mock them. He does this day in and day out, until finally one day the head waiter gets angry and decides to do something about it.

The Chinese head waiter enrolls in classes for

speech and elocution lessons. This takes months and months, and finally, after one year, he is ready to confront the Greek.

The next day, right on time, the Greek Restaurant owner goes into the Chinese restaurant. The head waiter comes over and says, "What can I get you today?"

True to form, the Greek says, "I'll have the *flied lice!*" laughing all the while, waiting to have it repeated.

To which the head waiter replies, "It is pronounced *fried rice*, you Gleek plick!"

Two Irishmen are fishing in a boat, on a lake. One Irishman hooks something; he reels it in and gets it in the boat. It is an old, rusted lamp. He brushes off the muck and soggy leaves and out pops a genie!

The genie says, "Wow, thanks a lot for saving me, I almost drowned down there. I'll tell you what, you get one wish—make it a good one—and I'm out of here!"

The Irishman thinks for a minute and says, "I want this whole lake filled with beer, as far as you can see, nothing but beer, no water. Make it Guinness!"

"That's it?" says the genie. "You got it!" He snaps his fingers, the whole lake is now filled with Guinness, and the genie disappears.

The other Irishman says to his friend, "Now what in the hell did you do that for? Now we have to piss in the boat!"

A guy calls in sick. His boss asks, "How sick are you?"

"I'm fucking a cooked, stuffed turkey—how sick is that!" comes the reply.

How are tightrope walking and a blow job
from Janet Reno the same?
In both cases it's best not to look down!

Why did the pervert cross the road?
His dick was in a chicken.

Why does a chicken coop have two doors?
*If it had four doors it would be
a chicken sedan.*

An old man is sitting on his porch when he sees a kid walk by with a roll of chicken wire in his arms. "Where you goin' with that chicken wire, boy?" he asks.

"I'm goin' to get me some chickens," says the boy.

"You can't catch chickens with chicken wire, boy," says the old man.

"I'm goin' to get me some chickens," says the boy as he keeps walking.

A half hour later, the boy passes the old man's house with his arms full of chickens, all clucking away, feathers everywhere. The old man just scratches his head.

An hour later, the boy passes the old man's

house with two big rolls of duct tape. The old man says, "Where you goin' with that duct tape, boy?"

"I'm goin' to get me some ducks!" the boy says.

"You can't catch ducks with duct tape!" the old man chuckles.

"I'm goin' to get me some ducks." And the boy walks on.

A half hour later, the boy walks by the old man's house with his arms full of ducks, all quacking, feathers everywhere. The old man just scratches his head.

One hour later the boy passes the old man's house with his arms full of pussy willows. The old man says, "Hold on, son, let me get my hat!"

Sherlock Holmes and Dr. Watson are in the wilderness, lying on the ground on their backs looking up at the sky. Holmes says to Watson, "Watson, look at the sky and tell me what you see."

"Well, Holmes, I see millions of stars," replies Watson.

"Very good, Watson," says Holmes. "But what does that tell you?"

"Well, Holmes, astronomically speaking, there are billions of bodies in the heavens, of which we are one," replies Watson.

"Very good, Watson," says Holmes. "But what does that tell you?"

"Well, Holmes, astrologically speaking, it tells

me that Saturn is in Leo. Time-wise, it appears to be a quarter past 3 A.M.," replied Watson.

"Very good, Watson," says Holmes. "But what does that tell you?"

"Well, Holmes, theologically, it is evident the Lord is all-powerful and we are small and insignificant," Watson tells Holmes.

"Very good, Watson," says Holmes. "But what does that tell you?"

"Well, Holmes, meteorologically, it is a clear, crisp night and it will be a beautiful day tomorrow?" Watson says, confused.

"Very good, Watson," says Holmes sternly. "*But what does that tell you*?"

"I don't know, Holmes, what does it tell you?" cries Watson, exasperated.

"It tells me, my dear Watson," says Holmes, "that someone has stolen the fucking tent!"

🍸

The Pope is in his bed, reading, when a thought pops in his head. He has never, in his whole life, experienced an orgasm. He quickly dismisses the notion, wondering how it got there in the first place, and continues reading. But it creeps back into his head again.

He gets out of bed and stands in front of his mirror. "I am old," he says to himself, "and I will die without ever knowing what an orgasm is or what it feels like." He decides to find out.

He puts on some old work clothes and a baseball cap, goes down the back stairs to the garage, careful not to be seen by anyone. He walks past the Popemobile and finds the gardener's old pickup truck. In the dead of night, the Pope drives the pickup truck out of the Vatican and into the country.

Five miles into the country, he takes a dirt road and drives five more miles and then stops the truck and gets out. It is pitch-black out—he can barely see the nose in front of his face. Confident that no one is around, he masturbates. He orgasms, waits fifteen minutes, and masturbates again. After he orgasms the second time, he climbs back in the truck and makes his way back to the Vatican. He sneaks back to his bedroom, takes off the old work clothes, and falls fast asleep.

The next morning he wakes up quite refreshed. He never slept like that before. It is the best sleep he has ever had. He sings while he is in the shower and dances around the bedroom while he is getting dressed for the day.

Full of energy and with a smile on his face, he is ready for the new day. As he walks to the door of the bedroom, he notices a manila envelope on the floor, obviously pushed under the door. He opens the envelope and pulls out an 8x10 glossy of himself with a baseball cap, his pants down around his ankles, and his hand wrapped around an enormous hard-on. Attached to the picture, there is a note which says, "I saw you last night. Send $100,000 to the address shown and I'll send you the negatives and the camera."

The Pope runs to his safe and opens it, pulls out $100,000, puts it in an envelope, addresses it, puts a stamp on it, and runs to the post office and mails it.

Two days later, a UPS truck pulls up to the Vatican, where the Pope is waiting anxiously. He grabs his package and runs up to his office, opens the package, and pulls out the negatives and the camera. He throws the negatives and the 8x10 glossy into the fireplace and waits until there is nothing but ashes. Then he takes the camera and places it on the mantel as a reminder to never do anything as stupid as that again.

One year later, the Japanese ambassador is visiting the Vatican. After a tour, the Pope takes the ambassador to his office for cigars and cognac. As they are smoking and drinking, the ambassador notices the camera on the mantel and reaches for it to get a closer look.

"Don't touch that camera!" yells the Pope. "It is very expensive!"

"How much you pay for camera?" asks the ambassador.

"That camera," says the Pope, "cost me $100,000!"

"Oh," says the Japanese ambassador. "They must have seen you coming!"

What do the Pope and the New York Jets
have in common?
*They are the only people who can get
sixty thousand people to yell 'Jesus Christ!'
in unison.*

Did you know that half of all Japanese eye
doctors have cataracts?
The other half drive Rincon Town Cars.

What do Japanese men do when they
have erections?
They vote.

A priest in a small country parish finds out
that the Pope is planning a surprise visit to his
church. The priest is excited and decides to do
some research on the Pope. He finds out that the
Pope loves local food and has a passion for fresh
fish, so he has his staff collect all the fresh vegeta-
bles from the local gardens while he goes fishing.
He hires a fishing guide and they head out to the
local lake.

While they are on the lake, the priest hooks a
big one. It takes him a half hour to reel it in, and

when he does, the fishing guide, who has never seen a fish that big in that lake, exclaims, "Will you look at that son of a bitch!"

Surprised, the priest says, "Please, I am a man of the cloth, such language offends me."

Embarrassed at his outburst, the guide tries to cover it up by saying, "No, you don't understand. That's the name of the fish. It's called a 'son of a bitch!'"

"Oh, I see," says the priest as he smiles at the big fish.

The priest goes back to the rectory, goes into the kitchen, and puts the fish on the counter. The altar boy comes in and the priest says to him proudly, "Will you look at this son of a bitch!"

The altar boy, taken aback, says, "Father, I've never heard language like that from you!"

"No, no," says the priest. "That's the name of the fish, a 'son of a bitch.'"

"Oh," says the altar boy, smiling. "I'll clean the son of a bitch!"

As the altar boy is cleaning the fish, the Mother Superior comes into the kitchen and the altar boy says, "Hey, Mother Superior, look at this son of a bitch!"

"Young man," says the Mother Superior sternly, "this is a house of the Lord and such language is not permitted!"

"Relax," says the priest to the Mother Superior, "that's the name of the fish. It's called a 'son of a bitch.'"

"Oh," says the Mother Superior. "Well, I'll cook the son of a bitch!"

The Pope arrives, and after a tour of the village and the church, the priest, the Mother Superior, the altar boy, and the guest of honor, the Pope, sit down for dinner.

All eyes are on the Pope as he eats. After two bites of the fish, he exclaims, "This is the best fish I have ever eaten!"

The priest says, "I caught the son of a bitch!"

The altar boy says, "I cleaned the son of a bitch!"

The Mother Superior says, "I cooked the son of a bitch!"

The Pope looks at all three and says with a smile, "Hey, you fuckers are all right!"

Did you hear about the new low-fat communion wafer? It's called "I can't believe it's not Jesus!"

An old couple die at the very same time and go to heaven. They are greeted by God himself. "Welcome! Come on in and enjoy!"

They walk down a beautiful path that passes a beautiful golf course. They both agree to play eighteen holes.

From the first hole on, after every shot, the old

man grumbles and swears terribly. He grumbles and swears on the front nine and he swears and grumbles on the back nine as well.

Finally the old lady can't take it anymore. She turns to her husband and says, "What is with you? You have either parred or birdied every hole here. When we were on Earth, you never broke one hundred! Why are you so pissed off?"

The old man looks at her and says, "If you hadn't put me on a low-fat, low-cholesterol diet, I'd have been here fifteen years ago!"

🍸

Why do golfers bring two pairs of shoes?
In case they get a hole in one.

I had to put this one in. I just had to.

🍸

A little boy runs home and says, "Daddy, Daddy, I got a part in the school play!"

"What part do you have?" asks the proud father.

"I play a Jewish husband!" says the smiling boy.

"Son," says the father, "go back and get a speaking role!"

🍺

A guy walks into his doctor's office and says, "Doc, I have a problem."

"What's the trouble?" asks the doctor.

The guy says, "My asshole is 16 1/2 inches in diameter and I'm getting worried."

The doctor says, "What?"

"My asshole," the guy says, "is 16 1/2 inches in diameter and I'm worried about it."

"Follow me," says the doctor, and they both go into the examining room. The doctor says, "Take off your clothes, bend over, and let's take a look."

The guy takes off his clothes and bends over. The doctor takes one look at the guy's butt and yells, "Holy shit! Your asshole is 16 1/2 inches wide! What the hell happened!"

The guy says, "Well, I was on safari in Africa and a bunch of rogue elephants attacked our group, and, well, one of the rogue elephants had sex with me."

"Now wait a minute," says the doctor. "I think it is common knowledge that, although it is long, an elephant's penis is not 16 1/2 inches in diameter."

"Well," says the guy, shyly, "he fingered me first."

What do you call a Jamaican proctologist?
Pokémon.

How do you get a roomful of blue-haired
old ladies to say "fuck"?
Yell out "Bingo!"

Quasimodo's mother brings out the wok.
"Oh boy," says Quasimodo, "I love Chinese food!"
"No, you idiot," says his mother, "I'm ironing your shirts!"

If you are dyslexic and cross-eyed, do you read right?

A cowboy goes into a bar and orders a drink. He has on a cowboy hat, cowboy shirt, and cowboy boots with spurs and chaps.

A woman sitting next to him asks, "Are you a real cowboy?"

"Well," the cowboy says, "I've been ranching all my life, riding horses, roping steer, branding cows, and mending fences. Yes, I'm a real cowboy. How about you?"

The woman says, "Well, when I wake up in the morning, I think of women. During breakfast, lunch, and dinner, I'm thinking of women. All day long and all night long, I'm thinking of women, and when I sleep, I dream of women. I'm a lesbian!" She finishes her drink, then leaves.

The cowboy is perplexed.

A couple comes in and sits down next to the cowboy. The woman says to the cowboy, "Are you a real cowboy?"

"Well," says the cowboy, "I thought I was a cowboy. Now I think I'm a lesbian!"

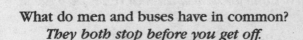

What do men and buses have in common?
They both stop before you get off.

Why did God create women?
He couldn't teach sheep to cook.

Why did God create men?
Because a dildo can't mow the lawn.

Hear about the gay guy who put a nicotine patch
on his dick?
He's down to two butts a day.

How do you know you are in a gay church?
Only half of the congregation is kneeling.

Why does a gay group want to buy the
New York Jets?
*Because the team has two tight ends and
forty players who suck.*

Here's one for all you animal rights activists ...

A baby seal walks into a club ...

A blind guy walks into a nightclub and starts swinging his dog around. The bouncer runs up to him and says, "What the hell are you doing?"

"Just looking around," says the blind guy.

Hear about the bartender who was married three times and all three wives died?

The first wife died of food poisoning. They found out it was poison mushrooms that killed her. The second wife died of food poisoning, too. Same thing, poison mushrooms.

The third wife died of a gunshot to the head. She wouldn't eat the fucking mushrooms!

What's the difference between a bitch
and a slut?
*A slut will fuck anybody. A bitch
will fuck anybody except you.*

In corporate offices, why do blondes have
a half hour for lunch instead of one hour
like everyone else?
It costs too much to retrain them.

What do puppy dogs and nearsighted
gynecologists have in common?
They both have wet noses.

An Irishman is walking down the street in
Dublin when he sees a crowd in front of a high-rise
building. He looks up and sees a guy standing on
the ledge of the tenth floor, obviously contemplat-
ing suicide. The Irishman rushes up and yells,
"Don't jump, think of your children!"

"I don't have any children!" yells the guy on the
ledge.

"Think of your wife!" the Irishman yells.

"I'm not married!" yells the guy.

"Think of your mother and father!" yells the
Irishman, undaunted.

"My parents died when I was young!" the guy
yells.

Frustrated, the Irishman yells, "Think of St.
Patrick!"

"Who's St. Patrick?" the guy on the ledge yells back.

"Jump, ya Protestant bastard, jump!" replies the
Irishman.

An American is in Ireland drinking in a pub.
After a few pints he yells, "I'll give a hundred dollars to the first guy that can drink twenty pints of

Guinness in a row, without stopping and without spilling a drop!"

A hush falls over the crowd. After a minute, a small, thin Irishman pushes his way through the crowd, approaches the American, and says, "I'll give it a try, but give me ten minutes and I'll be back to give it a go."

The American says, "All right, but if you are not back in ten minutes, the bet is off."

Sure enough, the Irishman returns exactly ten minutes later and says, "Set 'em up!"

The Irishman then proceeds to drink all twenty pints of Guinness, without stopping and without spilling a single drop.

Dumbfounded, the American hands over the hundred dollars and asks the Irishman, "To be honest, I didn't think you could drink them all. Tell me, where did you go for ten minutes?"

The Irishman burps and says, "I went to the pub across the street to see if I could do it!"

Evidently, the English tell Irish jokes, the Irish tell Scottish jokes, the Scottish tell Welsh jokes, and the Welsh say, "What's a joke?"

After a long journey, a German says, "I'm tired and thirsty, I must have a beer."

A Frenchman says, "I'm tired and thirsty, I must have some wine."

A Jewish man says, "Oy, I'm tired and thirsty, I must have diabetes!"

A doctor takes off his glasses, rubs his eyes, and says to his patient, "I have some bad news. You are dying of cancer. Now, I can help you through this with counseling. I have a one o'clock tee time, why don't you join me."

They go to the golf course, and on the first tee the patient runs into a few guys he knows and he tells them he is dying of AIDS. This goes on all afternoon, the patient telling everyone he knows that he is dying of AIDS.

Curious, the doctor asks, "Why are you telling everyone you are dying of AIDS when in fact you are dying of cancer?"

The guy looks at the doctor and in a low voice says, "I don't want any of my friends sleeping with my wife after I die."

What do you call eighty white guys
chasing one black guy?
The PGA Tour.

Why do Sicilians hate Jehovah's Witnesses?
Are you kidding, Sicilians hate all witnesses!

What do you call an Italian
who mixes cement with a fork?
A mortar-forker.

Two kids are in a hospital, in surgical gowns, sitting on their gurneys. "What are you here for?" asks the first kid.

"I'm here to get my tonsils removed," says the second kid.

"Don't worry," the first kid says. "I had my tonsils removed last year and you get all the ice cream you want!"

The second kid asks the first kid, "What are you here for?"

"I'm here for a circumcision," says the first kid.

"Oh my God," says the second kid. "I had that done when I was born! I didn't walk for a year!"

Do you know about the twins from Spain,
Juan and Emmal?
If you've seen Juan, you've seen Emmal.

Mickey Mouse and Minnie Mouse are standing before a judge in divorce court. The judge says to Mickey, "I don't understand. You want to divorce Minnie because she is crazy?"

"No," says Mickey, "I'm divorcing her because she's fucking Goofy!"

🍺

A New Yorker is driving in Northern Ireland and pulls into a gas station. He waits a few minutes and no one comes out, so he beeps his horn. The door opens a little and a guy sticks his head out.

"How about some gas?" says the New Yorker.

"I'm sorry, there is no gas," says the Irish attendant.

"Well, how about some oil?" says the New Yorker.

"No oil either, sorry," says the attendant.

"How about putting some water in the radiator?" says the New Yorker, slightly perturbed.

"Sorry, no water," says the attendant.

Now the New Yorker is pissed. "No gas, no oil, no water, what the hell are you here for?!"

"Well, actually," says the attendant in a low voice, "this is a front for the IRA."

The New Yorker looks at the attendant with disdain and says sarcastically, "Then why don't you blow up my tires!"

🍸

What do you call a smart pig in Ireland?
A cunning ham.

A nine-year-old boy is walking down the street when he hears a voice say, "Pssst, hey you!" He looks down and sees a frog on the sidewalk.

The frog says, "Kiss me now and I'll turn into a beautiful woman!" The boy picks up the frog, puts it in his pocket, and starts walking.

The frog sticks his head out of the pocket and says, "Hey, didn't you hear what I just said? I said, 'Kiss me now and I'll turn into a beautiful woman'!" The boy just shoves the frog back in his pocket and keeps walking.

The frog sticks his head out of the pocket again and says, "Hey, are you deaf? I said, 'KISS-ME-NOW-AND-I'LL-TURN-INTO-A-BEAUTIFUL-WOMAN'!"

The boy looks at the frog, shoves it back in his pocket, and says, "I'd rather have a talking frog!"

My youngest son, Michael, told me the next two jokes. He likes to pop popcorn without putting the lid on.

A UPS truck pulls up to a house. The driver gets out, goes to the back of the truck and gets a package, then walks to the front door of the house and knocks on the door.

A nine-year-old boy opens the door. He has a bottle of beer in one hand and a cigar in the other.

The UPS driver looks at the boy.

The boy looks at the UPS driver.

The driver asks, "Is your mother home?"

The boy takes a swig from the bottle of beer, takes a drag from the cigar, flicks the ash on the floor, blows the smoke in the driver's face, and says, "What do you think!"

A priest is walking down a street when he sees a little boy jumping up, trying to ring a doorbell. The boy says, "Hey, Father, can you help me out and ring the top doorbell?"

The priest rings the doorbell and asks, "Now what?"

"Run like hell!" says the boy.

Thanks, Mike, now put the book down and go to bed!

Albert Einstein has just finished cementing the sidewalk that leads to his front door and he goes inside. After a few minutes, he hears some noise outside, goes to the window, and sees some kids playing in the fresh cement.

Furious, he runs out and starts screaming and yelling at the kids. His neighbor hears this and says, "Albert, I thought you liked children!"

"I love children," says Einstein, "but in the abstract, not in the concrete!"

Three kids are at the Bronx Zoo, fighting. A security guard comes over and breaks it up. He asks the first kid, "What's going on here?"

The first kid says, "I was just trying to feed peanuts to the elephant."

The guard asks the second kid, "What were you doing?"

"I was trying to feed peanuts to the elephant, too," says the second kid.

"How about you?" the guard asks the third kid. "What were you doing?"

"Nothing," cries the third kid. "I'm Peanuts!"

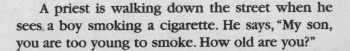

A priest is walking down the street when he sees a boy smoking a cigarette. He says, "My son, you are too young to smoke. How old are you?"

The boy says, "Six."

The priest says, "Six? When did you start smoking?"

The boy says, "Right after the first time I got laid."

Astounded, the priest says, "Right after the first time you got laid? When was that?"

"I don't remember," says the boy. "I was drunk."

A pirate walks into a bar with a ship's wheel attached to his dick. The bartender says, "What the hell is that?!"

The pirate says, "Arrrrr. It's a ship's wheel, and it's driving me nuts!"

Do you know the pirate alphabet?
A-Arrr, B-Arrrr, C-Arrrr . . .

How about a pirate eye chart?
R
RR
RRR
RRRR

Do you know why pirates like corn on the cob?
Because it's under a buccanneer.

Did you know that Cuba changed its
national anthem?
Now it's "Row, Row, Row Your Boat."

Two fish are in a tank. One fish says, "How do you drive this thing?"

A woman in a tight business suit is waiting for a bus. The bus arrives and she can't lift her leg to get on because her skirt is too tight. She reaches around to unzip it but it is still too tight so she reaches around and tries to unzip it some more.

All of a sudden, the guy behind her picks her up and puts her on the bus.

"How dare you!" she screams to the guy. "What the hell are you doing?"

"Well," says the guy, "after you unzipped my fly, I thought we're pretty good friends by now!"

What did the blonde get on her SATs?
Nail polish.

Why did the blonde climb over the glass wall?
To see what's on the other side.

If the mating call for a blonde is "I'm so drunk,"
what is the mating call for an ugly blonde?
"I said, I'm drunk!"

What job function does a blonde have
in an M&M's factory?
Proofreading.

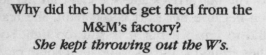

Why did the blonde get fired from the
M&M's factory?
She kept throwing out the W's.

Why are blonde jokes so short?
So brunettes can remember them.

The bar is three deep, I'm in the weeds, and Jill, my partner at the time, strolls over to me as if we're alone and tells me this joke, yelling the punch line at the top of her lungs. Needless to say, no one got a drink for the next ten minutes, we were laughing so hard!

Two nuns are driving down the road. They turn a corner and see a naked man standing in the middle of the road. The nun that's driving steps on the brakes and the car stops in front of the guy. She beeps the horn a little but the man doesn't move. She beeps a little longer and the guy still doesn't move. She leans on the horn and the guy doesn't even blink.

"What should I do?" she asks the nun in the passenger seat.

"Why don't you show him your cross?" the other nun replies.

The nun rolls down her window, sticks her head out and yells angrily, *"Get the fuck out of the road!"*

$$\text{\ding{38}}$$

A professor is conducting a study of the paranormal. He randomly sends out five thousand invitations for a seminar on paranormal behavior, and out of the five thousand, he receives two thousand favorable responses.

He gets all the people into an assembly hall and asks, "How many of you here have seen a ghost?"

Surprisingly, most of the people raise their hands.

"How many of you here," he continues, "have talked to a ghost?"

Only a few hands are raised.

"Has anyone here," the professor asks, "had sex with a ghost?"

No hands are raised, except for one old man way in the back of the hall, who puts his hand up.

"You mean to tell me, sir," asks the professor, "that you have actually had sex with a ghost?"

"*Ghost*?" says the old man. "Forget it, I thought you said, 'Goat'!"

A recent Physical Education graduate accepts a job to start and coach a swim team for a small college. None of the students are interested, so he puts a want ad in the local paper for swimming tryouts.

The next day, there is a knock on the coach's office door. He opens it and sees a man with no arms standing there.

"Can I help you?" asks the coach.

"I'm here to try out for the swim team," says the guy with no arms.

"I'm sorry," the coach apologizes, "but I need able-bodied swimmers."

"The ad says 'equal opportunity,' and I want a tryout!" demands the no-armed man.

To get it over with, the coach and the no-armed man head down to the Olympic-size swimming pool. The armless man jumps in and starts swimming using a beautiful dolphin kick. The coach pulls out a stopwatch and sees that the man with no arms is beating the times of bigger colleges in the state! He immediately signs the no-armed man and tells him to send anyone else he might know who swims.

The next day, the coach gets a knock on his office door, and when he opens it a man in a wheelchair, without legs, says, "I'm here for a tryout."

"I'm sorry—" the coach starts to say, but he is interrupted by the guy in the wheelchair. "My friend without arms told me to come for a tryout, and I'm better than he is!"

The coach wheels him down to the pool and the legless man slides off his wheelchair and slips into the pool, where he does a beautiful Australian crawl. The coach pulls out his stopwatch and sees that the guy with no legs is beating the time of the guy with no arms! He signs him on too, and tells him to send any friends that swim.

The next day, the coach is down at the pool office when he hears a knock on the door and opens it. He sees no one. But just as he is closing the door he hears a voice say, "Down here!" He looks down and sees a head. No body, just a head. "Can I help you?" he asks.

"I'm here to try out for the swim team," says the head.

"You've got to be kidding!" says the coach.

"Hey, my friend with no legs sent me, and I'm better than he is!" says the head.

"All right, all right," says the coach as he picks up the head and goes to the edge of the pool. "Ready?" he asks the head.

"Ready," says the head.

The coach drops the head in the water and it sinks to the bottom. He watches the head, but it doesn't move, only bubbles from it rise to the surface.

A minute goes by and the coach notices that the head is turning blue. Quickly he jumps in the water, grabs the head, brings it up, and places it on the side of the pool. "Are you all right?" he asks the coach. "What the hell happened?"

The head coughs, spits out water, and says, "What a hell of a time for a cramp!"

A grasshopper hops into a bar, looks around, and hops up on the bar counter. The bartender looks at the grasshopper and says, "There's a drink named after you."

The grasshopper looks at the bartender and says. "There's a drink named Fred?"

How do you make a dog drink?
Put it in a blender.

A wino is stumbling down the street with one foot on the sidewalk and the other in the gutter.

A cop pulls up and says to him, "I'm taking you in. You are obviously drunk."

"Offisher, are ya absholutely sure I'm drunk?" asks the wino.

"Yeah, I'm sure," says the cop. "Now let's go."

Breathing a sigh of relief, the wino says, "Thank goodnesh, I thought I was crippled!"

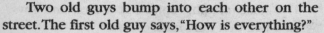

Two old guys bump into each other on the street. The first old guy says, "How is everything?"

The second old guy says, "Everything is great. I just bought a new hearing aid. It's high-tech, top-of-the-line, and very expensive."

"What kind is it?" asks the first old guy.

"It's four-thirty," says the second guy, looking at his watch.

What do you call a woman who always knows
where her husband is?
A widow.

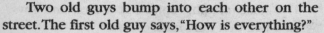

Why does a woman get her period once a month?
Because she deserves it.

How do you get a man to do sit-ups?
Put the TV remote control between his toes.

Why doesn't psychotherapy work on men?
They don't have to go back to their childhood.

A husband and wife are scuba diving and they get separated. The husband searches frantically until he runs out of air. He calls the Coast Guard and they immediately begin searching for her.

Two days later, the Coast Guard calls the husband and the captain says, "We've found your wife, but there's some good news and some bad news."

Bracing himself, the husband asks, "What's the bad news?"

"She's dead," says the captain.

"What the hell is the good news?" cries the husband.

"Well," says the captain, "When we pulled her out of the water, she had three good-sized lobsters and seven crabs attached to her gear."

"What's so good about that?" demands the husband.

"We are going to bring her up again tomorrow!" says the captain.

A male crab and a female lobster are dating, but they are hiding it from their parents because of the obvious reasons. Eventually the lobster gets tired of all the secrecy and she tells her father, who is furious and forbids her to see the crab again.

"But why can't I see the crab again? We're in love!" the lobster cries.

"Because," says the father, trying to search for a plausible answer, "crabs walk sideways and we walk straight!"

"Please, Father," she begs. "Just meet him once and I'm sure you will change your mind."

The father finally agrees to meet the crab and she runs out to tell him the good news.

The crab is so excited that he practices walking straight. He practices and practices and practices until, finally, he can walk straight. He walks all the way to the lobster's house as straight as he can.

The father sees him coming and yells to his daughter, "Hey, here comes that crab and he's drunk!"

What do you call a fish with no eye?
Fsh.

Remember when you were a kid and you used to blow bubbles?
I saw him yesterday and he says hello.

If you are having sex with two women and one
more woman walks in, what do you have?
Divorce proceedings.

A stockbroker is busted for inside trading, con-
victed, and sent to prison. As he gets to his cell, his
worst fear is there to greet him. His cellmate, a six-
foot-five, three-hundred-pound black man, says,
"You want to be the husband or do you want to be
the wife?"

The stockbroker weighs the options. He figures it is better to give than to receive so he says,
"I'll be the husband."

The six-foot-five, three-hundred-pound sweaty
black man says, "Then why don't you be a good
husband and suck your wife's dick!"

In Maine, Moosehead is a beer. In West Virginia,
it's a misdemeanor.

What's Ebonic for transvestite?
Susan B. Anthony.

What is a Jewish woman's dream house?
Seven rooms, no kitchen, no bedroom.

What's pink and hard in the morning?
The Financial Times *crossword puzzle.*

A scratch golfer hits his ball three hundred yards straight down the fairway, and it hits a sprinkler and careens off into the woods. He finds the ball, but it is surrounded by trees. He's pissed, says what the hell, grabs his nine-iron, and hits the ball as hard as he can. It bounces off a tree back at the golfer's head and kills him.

He arrives in heaven, and God himself is at the Pearly Gates to greet him. Looking up his records, God sees that the guy golfs and says, "Are you any good?"

The golfer looks at God and says, "I got here in two, didn't I?"

How do you know when you are a loser?
When a nymphomaniac says,
"Let's just be friends."

What's the difference between a woman
and a battery?
A battery always has a positive side.

🍸

What does a man consider a seven-course meal?
A hot dog and a six-pack of beer.

🍺

Three guys are interviewing for one job. Now,
the boss doesn't have any ears and decides to hire
the first person who doesn't say anything about it.
After the first interview, he asks, "Do you notice
anything odd about me?"

The first guy is rude and says, "Yeah, you don't
have any fucking ears."

The boss says, "Send in the next applicant on
your way out."

After the second guy interviews, the boss asks
the same question: "Do you notice anything odd
about me?"

The second guy is polite and says, "Well, sir, I
notice that, through some affliction, you are missing your ears."

The boss says, "Thank you, send in the next
applicant."

On the way out, the second guy says to the
third guy, "Whatever you do, don't say anything
about his ears."

After the third guy gives a great interview, the boss asks, "Do you notice anything odd about me?"

"Yes, I do," says the third guy. "You are wearing contact lenses."

The boss says, "Very good, you are hired. By the way, how did you know I'm wearing contacts?"

"Because," the third guy says, "if you had any ears, you would be wearing fucking glasses!"

I'm taking a flight out of La Guardia to Tampa so I can visit with my friend Hutch and his family for a long weekend. I have to connect in Memphis, and I learn when I get there that the connecting flight to Tampa is delayed by one hour.

So what do I do? Being a good bartender, I find the nearest bar. It is late, no one is in the bar but me and the bartender, and she is slowly (union job) getting ready to close. I have about forty-five minutes, she says.

So I'm sitting there, eating some peanuts that are in bowls along the bar and listening to soft music as I watch soundless TV, drinking a beer, with another on ice—ready when I am.

Out of nowhere, I hear a voice say, "Hey, nice shirt." I turn around to see where the voice came from, but no one is there. The bartender is in the corner stacking glasses, the music is low, and no sound is coming from the TV, so I figure that either I'm hearing things, or my fun times from the sixties are catching up with me.

I continue to eat more peanuts, drink the other beer that was on ice, listen to soft music, and watch soundless TV. Then the same voice says, "Hey, nice shoes."

Now, I *know* I heard that! Again, no one is around. It didn't come from the low music, it didn't come from the soundless TV, and the bartender is still in the corner stacking glasses. I call her over and ask, "Did you say something to me?"

"No, I didn't say anything to you," she says. "What happened?"

"Well," I say, "someone said, 'Nice shirt,' and a few minutes later the same voice said, 'Nice shoes.' I was wondering if you said it."

"Oh," she says, "I know what it was."

"What was it?" I ask, hoping I wasn't having a senior moment early in my young life.

"It's the peanuts," she says with a smile. "They're complimentary."

The Carrot family are having a fun day in Central Park. They leave the park at dusk to go home and as they cross 5th Avenue, a cab goes out of control and hits the father carrot. An ambulance arrives and takes him off to the hospital, followed by his family.

After five hours of surgery, the doctor comes out to speak with the mother carrot.

"How is he? Will he live?" asks the mother carrot.

"He'll live," says the doctor, "but he'll be a vegetable for the rest of his life."

Why don't cannibals eat clowns?
Because they taste funny.

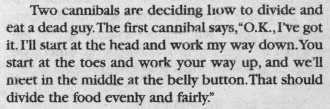

Two cannibals are deciding how to divide and eat a dead guy. The first cannibal says, "O.K., I've got it. I'll start at the head and work my way down. You start at the toes and work your way up, and we'll meet in the middle at the belly button. That should divide the food evenly and fairly."

After a few minutes, the first cannibal asks the second cannibal, "How are you doing?"

The second cannibal says, "I'm having a ball!"

The first cannibal says, "Hey, slow down! You're eating too fast!"

What did the cannibal get when he was
late for dinner?
The cold shoulder.

Did you hear about the cannibal that ordered a pizza with everybody on it?

How about the cannibal's recipe book? *How to Serve Your Fellow Man*.

After the St. Patrick's Day Parade, a drunk staggers down 5th Avenue, lurches into St. Patrick's Cathedral and sways down the aisle, bumping into pew after pew. Finally, he stumbles into the confessional. A priest, who has been watching him, figures that he needs help and enters the other side of the confessional. "How may I help you, my son?" he asks.

Silence from the other side.

The priest asks again, "May I help you, my son?"

"Yeah," comes the drunk's voice from behind the partition. "You got any toilet paper on your side?"

Why is there a St. Paddy's Day Parade?
So a half a million Jews can watch the help go by.

What do you call a wandering nun?
A Roman Catholic.

♢

The Last Supper. Jesus looks at his disciples and says, "Soon, one of you will betray me."

All the disciples look at one another in shock. Paul asks, "Is it me, Jesus? Will I betray you?"

"No, Paul," Jesus says. "It is not you."

Matthew asks, "Is it me, Jesus? Will I betray you?"

"No, Matthew, it is not you," Jesus answers.

John asks the same question. "Is it me, Jesus, will I betray you?"

"No, John," Jesus says. "It is not you."

All the rest of the disciples ask the same question, Judas being the last one. "Is it me, Jesus?" he asks.

In a mocking, high-pitched voice, Jesus answers, *"Is it me, Jesus, is it me, Jesus . . . ?"*

♢

Or how about this one . . .

Jesus and his disciples have just finished the Last Supper. The head waiter comes over and hands the bill to Jesus, who passes it to the nearest disciple. The disciple in turn passes the bill to the one next to him, and this continues until it reaches Judas.

Judas takes one look at the bill and says, "Shit! Where am I supposed to get thirty silver pieces?"

What happened to Jesus when he went
to Mount Olive?
Popeye beat the shit out of him.

A Southern Baptist minister finds out that the town drunk has never been baptized. He gathers the townspeople together, grabs the drunk, and they all head to the river. There, the minister says a few words and dunks the head of the drunk into the water for ten seconds. Pulling the drunk's head out of the water, the minister asks, "Have you found Jesus?"

The drunk coughs and says, "No!"

The minister dunks his head again for twenty seconds, pulls him up, and asks again, "Have you found Jesus?"

The drunk coughs a couple of times and says, "No!"

Undaunted, the minister dunks the drunk's head in the water and holds him under for a whole minute. Finally, he pulls the drunk's head out of the water and asks, "Have you found Jesus!?"

The drunk coughs, sputters, spits out some water, and says, "No! Are you sure this is where he went under?"

Yeshiva University's rowing team cannot, no matter how hard they try, win. In a word, they suck. So the university sends the captain of the team to Harvard to scout their rowing team to learn and see what they are doing wrong. After three weeks, he comes back and says to the coach, "I figured out what we were doing wrong!"

"Great!" says the coach. "What did you find out?"

"There are eight men rowing and only one man yelling!" says the captain.

Why does the Easter Bunny give away
Easter eggs?
He doesn't want anyone to know he's
fucking chickens.

A woman walks into a bank, goes up to the teller, and says, "I want to open a fucking savings account!"

The teller blinks and says, "Excuse me?"

"I said," the woman says, "I want to open a fucking savings account!"

"You are very rude," says the teller. "There is no need to use that kind of language." With that, she goes and gets the bank manager.

The bank manager comes back with the teller and asks the woman, "What seems to be the problem?"

"Look," the woman says, "I just hit the lottery for ten million dollars and I just want to open up a fucking savings account!"

The manager looks at the teller and then at the woman and says, "And this bitch is giving you a hard time?"

What is it when a man talks dirty to a woman?
Sexual harassment.
What is it when a woman talks dirty to a man?
$3.99 a minute.

Did you hear about the Alabama quarter? It's two nickels and a dime, glued together.

Kentucky changed its state motto to . . .
Welcome to Kentucky: fifteen million people, ten last names!

Why doesn't Mexico have an Olympic team?
Because everybody who can run, jump, and swim is already in the U.S.

How can you tell when a Mexican woman
has been sucking cock?
She spits out feathers.

Hear about the Polish gang member who got in
a rumble? He pulled out his razor, but couldn't find
anywhere to plug it in.

Why did God give women one more brain cell
than horses?
So they won't shit during parades.

Why did God give men one more brain cell
than dogs?
*So they won't hump women's legs
at cocktail parties.*

A 2002 white stretch limousine pulls up to a stoplight right next to a 1955 Oldsmobile 98 Starfire, mint condition. The man in the back of the limousine pushes a button and his window rolls down.

He says to the Oldsmobile driver, "Hey, nice car."

The guy in the Olds says, "Thanks. I have a TV in here, cable ready."

Not to be outdone, the man in the limo says, "I have a TV, a VCR, and a satellite dish."

"I have a microwave oven," says the guy in the Olds.

"I have a convection oven with a full-time chef," says the man in the limo.

"I have a four-poster brass bed!" the guy in the Olds says as the light changes and he takes off.

Furious, the man in the limo picks up the phone and calls his driver. "James, I want you to take this limousine to the customizing shop and have them install a four-poster brass bed with a canopy, a bearskin rug, and a fireplace. I don't care what it costs and I want it tomorrow!"

The next day, with the limousine the way he

wants it, the man goes out to look for the Oldsmobile. After four hours of searching, he finally finds the Olds parked on the side of the road with all its windows fogged up. He gets out of the limo and knocks on the window of the Olds. No answer.

He knocks again. Still no answer.

He knocks on the window a third time, longer and harder. Finally, the window rolls down and the guy in the Olds shouts, "What the hell do you want?"

The man from the limousine says proudly, "I just put in a four-poster brass bed with a canopy, a bearskin rug, and a fireplace!"

The guy in the Oldsmobile looks at the man angrily and says, "You got me out of the Jacuzzi to tell me that?"

Only a man would buy a $500 car and put a $4,000 stereo in it!

A blonde wanted to change her image, so she decided to buy a new car that would set her apart from all other blondes. At the car dealer, she was about to give up when she spotted a beautifully restored Jaguar XK-140 convertible. She bought it on the spot.

She drove it off the lot and headed for the country, her long blonde hair flowing in the wind, and music blaring from the radio. It was a gorgeous day.

Then, all of a sudden, the engine conked out and the Jaguar slowly coasted to a stop. She turned the key, but the car wouldn't start. Knowing her limitations, she called Triple A auto club and waited for the tow truck. After ten minutes the truck arrived and the mechanic asked, "What seems to be the problem?"

"Well," said the blonde, "It just sputtered and stopped.

"Let me take a look," said the mechanic, and after fifteen minutes the engine was purring like a cat again.

"Thank goodness," said the blonde. "What was the matter?"

"Simple, really," said the mechanic. "Just crap in the carburetor."

Looking shocked, the blonde asked, "Oh. How many times a week do I have to do that?"

🍸

And speaking of blondes ...

Why do blondes like BMWs?
Because they can't spell "Chevrolet."

🍸

What's a brunette's mating call?
"Has that blonde gone yet?"

What's the mating call of a redhead?
"Next!"

Do not tell this joke at the dinner table!

A couple get married and head off to the lake to stay in the honeymoon cabin. The next morning the caretaker of the cabins notices the man fishing from the honeymoon cabin's dock. Curious, he walks up to him and says, "How's the fishing?"

"Great," says the man, pointing to a bucket with three fish in it.

"You're in the honeymoon cabin, aren't you?" asks the caretaker.

"Yep," says the man.

"Well," says the caretaker, "it's none of my business, but shouldn't you be in there with your bride consummating the marriage?"

"She has gonorrhea," says the man.

"Well," says the caretaker, "it's none of my business, but there is always oral sex."

"Nope, she has pyorrhea," says the man.

"Well, it's none of my business, but what about anal sex?" asks the caretaker.

"Nope, she has diarrhea," says the man.

"Now wait a minute," says the caretaker. "It's none of my business, but if she had gonorrhea, pyorrhea, and diarrhea, why on earth did you marry her?"

"She has worms, too," says the man.

What did the blonde say to the physicist?
"I love nuclear fission. What do you use for bait?"

What's the difference between a man and a catfish?
One is a bottom-feeding scumsucker, and the other is a fish.

Why are women like a map of the world?
Before 16, they are like Africa, unexplored; 16 to 25, like North America, plenty of natural resources with room for western expansion; 25 to 40, like South America, hot and exotic; 40 to 55, like Europe, battle-scarred and worn, but still points of interest; 55 and on, like Antarctica—everyone knows it's there, but who gives a shit!

An old man goes to his doctor. "Doc, you have to help me!" he yells.

"What seems to be the problem?" asks the doctor.

"Doc," the old man shouts, "I accidentally pushed my hearing aid in too far. It hurts and I can't hear a thing. You gotta get it out!"

The doctor reaches in his ear with the forceps and pulls out the object. "This isn't your hearing aid, it's a suppository," he says in disbelief.

"Oh," says the old man as he turns around and drops his pants. "Could you see if my hearing aid is in here?"

⚇

My college philosophy professor once asked, "If an old man farts and his hearing aid is up his ass, does he hear it?"

🍺

Why are men like laxatives?
They both irritate the shit out of you.

⚇

What's the difference between purple and pink?
The grip.

🍺

Two guys, Chuck and Bob, go duck hunting. Chuck brings his new retriever and can't wait to show Bob how unique the dog is at retrieving ducks.

A duck flies over, Bob shoots it, and the duck falls in the water. Chuck sends his dog to retrieve it. The dog walks on top of the water, gets the duck, and walks on top of the water back to the duck blind, dropping the duck at Bob's feet. Bob doesn't say a word.

Another duck flies by and Chuck shoots it. The dog walks on top of the water, gets the duck, and walks on top of the water back to the duck blind, dropping the duck at Chuck's feet. Again, Bob says nothing.

This goes on all morning—the dog walks on top of the water, gets the duck, and walks on top of the water back to the duck blind, dropping the duck at the feet of whoever shot it. Finally, Chuck can't take it anymore and asks Bob, "Do you notice anything unusual about my dog?"

Bob looks at Chuck and says, "Yeah, your dog can't swim."

What's the difference between a Northern zoo
and a Southern zoo?
*The Northern zoo has the name of the animal
and the species in Latin. The Southern zoo has
the name of the animal and the recipe.*

🍸

What's the difference between a Northern
fairy tale and a Southern fairy tale?
*A Northern fairy tale begins with, "Once upon
a time . . ." A Southern fairy tale begins with,
"Y'all ain't gonna believe this shit . . ."*

🍸

A lion is up on a hill screwing the hell out of a
zebra. All of a sudden, the lion sees Mrs. Lion coming up the hill. He says to the zebra, "Quick, act like
I'm killing you!"

🍺

Two cows are talking. One cow says to the
other cow, "Hey, what do you know about this 'mad
cow disease' they are having over in England? How
do you think it will affect us?"
The other cow says, "I don't know what you
are talking about. I'm a duck!"

🍸

After a few too many, a guy leaves the local pub, sneaks into his house, tiptoes up the stairs into the bedroom, slips under the covers of his marital bed, and starts going down.

After a while of doing this, all of the beer gets to him and he has to take a piss. He quietly goes to the bathroom and sees his wife sitting on the bowl. Confused, the guy says, "What are you doing here?"

"Shhh," the wife says. "You'll wake up my mother!"

Two Irishmen walk out of a bar . . .
Hey, it could happen!

Three blondes walk into a bar . . .
You'd think one of them might have seen it!

Hear about the blonde that got an AM radio?
It took her a month to realize she could play it at night.

How are men and parking spots alike?
The good ones are always taken and the ones that are left are all handicapped.

A midget with a harelip wants to buy a horse. He goes to the nearest horse farm and looks around. The farmer comes over and asks, "Can I help you?"

"Yeth," says the midget, pointing to a horse. "I want to thee that horth." The farmer walks with the midget to the horse.

"I want to thee it'th mane," says the midget.

The farmer picks him up so he can touch the horse's mane, puts him back down and says, "Anything else?"

The midget says, "I want to thee it'th eyeth."

The farmer picks him up again, shows him the horse's eyes, and puts him down. "Anything else?" he asks.

"Yeth," says the midget, "I want to thee it'th earth."

The farmer picks up the midget, shows him the horse's ears, and puts him back down. "Anything else?" he asks.

"Yeth," says the midget, "I want to thee it'th back."

At this point, the farmer is getting pissed. He quickly picks up the midget, shows him the horse's back, and quickly puts him back down. "Anything else?" asks the agitated farmer.

"Yeth," says the midget, "I want to thee it twat."

Now the farmer is really pissed off. He picks up the midget, lifts the horse's tail, and shoves his face in the horse's ass. After a minute, he puts the midget on the ground and says angrily, "How was that!"

The harelipped midget sputters and spits and says, "Well, that wath fine, but I really want to thee it run and gallop!"

A midget walks up to a tall blonde in a bar and says. "Hey, what do you say to a little fuck?"

She looks at him and says, "Hello, you little fuck!"

What do you get when you cross a pygmy
with a whore?
You get a little fucker this big!
(use your fingers)

Why do cavemen pull their women around
by the hair?
Because if they pulled them around by their
feet, they'd fill up with mud.

How do you change a woman's mind?
Buy her another drink.

What's a man's idea of foreplay?
A half hour of begging.

A guy walks into a bar, sits down, and notices a horse behind the bar. The horse trots over and says, "What can I get you?"

The guy asks for a beer. The horse gets the beer, opens it, and brings it to the guy, then trots to the other end of the bar to another customer.

The guy sips his beer, but can't take his eyes off the horse. Every time the horse looks at the guy, the guy is looking at the horse.

This is bugging the horse, so he trots over to the guy and says, "What's the matter, never seen a horse behind a bar before?"

"No," says the guy, "I can't say that I have."

"Well," says the horse, "Not only am I the bartender, but I'm the owner of this bar as well. I bought it last week. You got a problem with that?"

"No, no, not at all," says the guy, "I'm surprised the parrot sold it."

Do you know why the big bad wolf
got arrested?
One of the pigs squealed.

What does a snail say while riding on top
of a turtle?
"Weeeeeeeeeeeeeee!"

A snail gets mugged by two turtles. The cops
show up and asks him what happened. The snail
says, "I don't know, it happened so fast!"

A pregnant wife and her husband are in bed.
She is reading, he is asleep. The wife wakes up her
husband and says, "I want some escargots."

The husband says, "What?"

"Escargots!" she says. "You know, snails! I want
some snails!"

The husband looks at her and pleads, "Ah,
come on, honey, the refrigerator is full of food in
case you get cravings—pickles, ice cream, sweets,
everything you like is in the kitchen. What's up
with the snails?"

"I want snails!" she screams. "Now!"

"All right, all right," the husband says. "But
where am I going to get snails this time of night?"

"There is a gourmet deli," she says. "Six blocks
from here, open all night."

The husband gets out of bed, gets dressed, and
goes to the deli. He buys a bag full of fresh snails
and starts to walk back, but on the way he passes

the local pub and sees his buddies in the window, waving for him to come in. He goes in and says he can only stay for one drink.

Well, you know guys, one drink leads to another, and the next thing you know it is 4 A.M. The guy grabs the bag of snails and runs home.

At the top of the stairs to the apartment, he drops the bag and all the snails fall out and some roll down the stairs. At that moment, the door opens and the wife yells, "Where the hell have you been?"

The guy looks at the snails in the hall and down the stairs, then looks at his wife, and with a gesture of his arm he says, "Come on, let's go, we're almost there!"

An old woman is lonely and decides to buy a parrot. She goes down to the only pet store in town and as she walks in the door, a parrot, in its cage near the entrance, says, "Hello." She thinks that's wonderful and buys the parrot.

That night, as she is getting undressed, the parrot says, "Nice legs!" She stops, turns, and looks at the parrot.

The parrot says, "Nice ass, too!"

The old woman walks up to the cage and says sternly, "What did you say?"

The parrot says, "Wanna fuck?"

The old woman is so incensed that she grabs the parrot by the throat, brings him into the kitchen, opens the freezer door, throws him in the freezer, and closes the door. After twenty minutes, she opens the freezer door and pulls the parrot out and says, "Have you learned your lesson?"

The parrot, with its whole body shivering and its beak full of frost, says, "Oh, yes, ma'am, I've learned my lesson very well and I must apologize that I have offended you with my language and I ask for your forgiveness, but may I ask a question of you?"

"Yes, you may," says the old woman, softening a bit. "What is your question?"

"May I ask," says the parrot, "what the turkey said to you?"

A man is flying first class from New York to Los Angeles and is lucky enough to be seated next to a beautiful woman. After takeoff, the woman opens a book that catches the man's eye. It is a manual about sexual statistics.

The man says, "Excuse me, but what is that book you are reading?"

"Oh," says the woman, "it is a very interesting book about sexual statistics. It states that Native Americans, on average, have the longest penis and that, on average, Jewish men have the biggest in diameter."

"That's fascinating," says the man. "What is your name?"

"My name is Heather," says the woman. "What's yours?"

"Schwartz, Tonto Schwartz," says the man.

This is so old, Vaudeville was an infant!

A guy calls up the law firm of Schwartz, Schwartz, Schwartz and Schwartz. A voice on the other end says, "Thank you for calling Schwartz, Schwartz, Schwartz and Schwartz, how can I help you?"

"I'd like to speak to Mr. Schwartz," the guy says.

The voice says, "He's in a meeting right now."

"Well," says the man, "Let me speak to Mr. Schwartz."

"I'm sorry, he's out to lunch," says the voice.

"Then," says the man, "Let me speak to Mr. Schwartz."

"He is with a client, I'm sorry," says the voice.

"Well, then," says the man, "I'd like to speak to Mr. Schwartz."

"Speaking," says the voice.

What is fourteen inches long and hangs
in front of an asshole?
A lawyer's tie.

What's the difference between a
woman lawyer and a pit bull?
Lipstick.

A man walks into a lawyer's office and inquires about the lawyer's rates.

"Fifty dollars for three questions," replies the lawyer.

"Isn't that awfully steep?" asks the man.

"Yes," says the lawyer. "And what was your third question?"

🍺

A man loses his job, his house is foreclosed, and his wife leaves him, taking all his money along with the children. He is destitute. He must find out what the meaning of life is. He must seek out the High Lama.

It takes him three years to reach Nepal and seven more months to finally find the Shrine of the High Lama. When he gets there he is told to wait two more weeks, since the High Lama cannot see him earlier.

Two weeks go by, and in his tattered clothes, unshaven and unwashed, near starvation and humbled, he stands before the High Lama.

"Life," says the High Lama, "is like a fountain."

"*What*!?!?" yells the guy incredulously. "I lose my job, my house, my wife, my children, and my money, I travel for three years and seven months to get here, then I'm told to wait for two weeks, and finally all you say is life is like a fucking fountain?!"

"Life is not like a fountain?" says the High Lama.

🍸

A teacher is teaching her class about morals. She gives a few examples and tells the students to bring in a story that has a moral to it. The next day she asks, "Who has a story with a moral to it?"

Everyone in the class raises their hands, much to the teacher's delight. "Mary, please tell us your story," she says.

Little Mary stands up and says, "I live on a farm and one of my chores is to collect some eggs from the chicken coop and bring them up to the farmhouse before I go to school.

"Well," Mary continues, "one day I went to the chicken coop, collected all the eggs and put them in my basket, and as I was walking to the farmhouse my dog Muffy jumped up on me and I dropped the basket and all the eggs broke."

"I'm sorry to hear that, Mary," says the teacher. "But what is the moral to the story?"

"Don't put all of your eggs in one basket," Mary says.

"Very good, Mary," says the teacher. "Now, who's next?"

Everyone has their turn, and finally little Johnny is the last one. "Johnny, tell us your story," says the teacher.

Johnny stands up and says, "My daddy is a Vietnam War veteran and when he was in the war, all he had was three bullets, a hand grenade, a bayonet, and a bottle of whiskey.

"Well, one day," Johnny continues, "my daddy looked up from his foxhole and saw three VC coming right at him, so he took a swig from the whiskey bottle, aimed his rifle, and killed all the three VC with the three bullets. Then ten more VC charged him. He took a bigger swig of whiskey, pulled the pin of the grenade, threw it, and killed all ten VC. Then when the smoke cleared, he saw twenty more VC coming right at him, so he finished the bottle of whiskey, fixed the bayonet on his rifle, and killed all twenty of the VC with the bayonet and hand-to-hand combat, and he is alive to tell the story, to this day."

"That's fascinating, Johnny," says the teacher. "What is the moral of the story?"

Johnny proudly says, "Don't fuck with my daddy when he's been drinking!"

A farmer thinks it's time to retire the old rooster and buys a younger one. The young rooster walks up to the old one and says, "O.K., time to go, old-timer, young stud is here!"

"Relax, youngster," says the old rooster. "I'm not going anywhere. I have a few more good years in me."

"Don't give me a hard time," says the young rooster. "It's time for the old to step aside and the young to take over, so take a hike!"

"I'll tell you what," says the old rooster, "I'll race you around the farmhouse. Whoever wins gets domain of the chicken coop, and the loser leaves the farm."

"You know I'm going to beat you," says the young rooster, "so, just to be fair, I'll give you a head start."

They line up behind the farmhouse, a chicken says "Go," and the old rooster starts running. Fifteen seconds later, the young rooster takes off after him. They round the front of the farmhouse and the young rooster is twelve inches behind the old rooster and gaining fast.

The farmer, sitting on the porch, sees what's going on, grabs his shotgun, and blows the young rooster to bits.

His wife says, "What did you do that for?"

The farmer shakes his head and says, "Third damned gay rooster I bought this week!"

A well-dressed woman is shopping on Madison Avenue. A bum walks up to her and says, "I haven't eaten anything in four days."

She looks at him and says, "God, I wish I had your willpower!"

Why do brides wear white at their wedding?
*So the dishwasher matches the rest
of the appliances.*

How many men does it take to screw in
a lightbulb?
One: men will screw anything.

*This is from my oldest son, Matt, who is a
computer engineer. When Matt was a toddler, I
used to put his clothes on backwards and send
him off to preschool as if nothing was wrong.*

How many computer engineers does it take
to screw in a lightbulb?
*FiV5 One y7 Uujy The bUL8 Anv foUx
to eJHGF The eXPEfkncdE!*

*One night a couple of Swedes came in the bar
and gave me this gem. Unfortunately, they never
translated it. If anyone knows what it means,
please write in and tell me.*

Varfor har norrmannen pyjamas de
aker motorcykel?
De ligger i kurvorna!

*My friend Doyle says reality is for people who
can't handle drugs!*

A piano player walks by a bar with a sign in the window that says, "Piano player wanted." He walks in and asks for an audition.

He plays a beautiful piece that moves the manager to tears. The manager asks, "What's the name of that song?"

The piano player says, "It is an original piece titled, 'I fucked my girlfriend and made her scream.'"

The manager asks to hear another song. The piano player plays another equally beautiful piece. The manager asks, "What's the name of that one?"

The piano player says, "Another original titled, 'When we finished fucking, I wiped my dick on the curtains.'"

The manager says, "Listen, I'll hire you, but you've got to promise not to tell anyone what the names of the songs are. It might offend my clientele."

The piano player agrees, and he starts playing that night. Everything is going very well, the customers are really enjoying the songs. After an hour, the piano player takes a break and goes to the bathroom. When he comes out, a customer comes up to him and says, "Do you know your fly is open and your dick is hanging out?"

"Know it?" says the piano player. "I wrote it!"

🍸

One morning, the lion, King of Beasts, wakes up feeling mean. He is walking about, corners a small monkey, and roars, "Who is the mightiest of all animals?!"

The monkey trembles and says, "You are, mighty lion!" and scampers up a tree.

The lion continues along and comes up to a frightened gazelle. "Who is the mightiest of all animals?!" he roars.

The gazelle stammers, "Oh, great lion, you are the mightiest of all animals!" and runs away.

Now the lion is really full of himself, and he swaggers up to an elephant and roars, "Who is the mightiest of all animals?!"

The elephant grabs the lion with its trunk, slams him against a tree ten times, and then throws him twenty yards away.

The lion staggers to his feet, full of pain, and says to the elephant. "Gee, just because you don't know the answer, you don't have to get so angry!"

What do you do with an elephant
that has three balls?
You walk him and pitch to the giraffe.

How do you stop a rhinoceros from charging?
Take away its credit card.

Why doesn't Santa Claus have any children?
*Because he only comes once a year,
and when he does, it's down the chimney.*

Why is Santa Claus so jolly?
He knows where all the bad girls live.

What do all the female reindeer do
when Santa takes the male reindeer out
on Christmas Eve?
They go into town and blow a few bucks.

How is Christmas like a day at the office?
*You do all the work and the fat man in the suit
gets all the credit.*

There are eight reindeer, and Rudolf makes
nine, but do you know about the tenth reindeer,
Olive? You know, "Olive, the other reindeer/used
to laugh and call him names."

What's the difference between snowmen
and snowladies?
Snowballs.

Why did the woman get a tattoo of a turkey
on the inside of one thigh and a tattoo of
Santa Claus on the inside of her other thigh?
*For her husband who always complains
that there's nothing to eat between
Thanksgiving and Christmas.*

What do married couples buy Vaseline for?
Seventy-nine cents a jar.

If one is love and two is hate,
what's three and four?
Seven.

There are three kinds of people in the world:
those who can count and those who can't.

It was found, in a recent study, that five out of four high school students can't do fractions.

How do you know when you are *really* ugly?
Dogs hump your leg with their eyes closed.

Why did God create alcohol?
So ugly people will have a chance to have sex, too.

"You know that woman, Eve, you created for me?" Adam says to God. "What a great cook! Breakfast, lunch, and dinner, anything I want to eat, she cooks it for me and cooks it very well!"

"I made her that way," God says, "so you will like her."

Then Adam says, "And good-looking, too! She is absolutely gorgeous! I can't keep my eyes off her!"

"I made her that way," God says, "so you will like her."

"And sex!" Adam continues. "She is just fabulous in bed! Anything I want her to do, she does, and she does it great!"

"I made her that way," God says, "so you will like her."

"But, there is one problem," Adam says. "She is dumber than a rock! She is very stupid and not too bright, either!"

"I made her that way," God says, "so she will like you."

How do you know Jesus wasn't Italian?
If he was, you wouldn't find three wise men and a virgin.

God and Moses are playing a round of golf. Moses tees off and his ball lands in the pond in front of the green. He walks to the pond, raises his arms, the water parts, he walks in and chips out onto the green.

God tees off. His ball sails past the pond, past the green, and before it hits the ground an eagle flies by, grabs the ball with its talons, realizes that the ball is not food, circles over the pond, and drops the ball. The ball hits a turtle in the pond, bounces onto the green, and rolls into the cup for a hole in one.

Moses walks up to God and says, "Look, are you going to play golf, or are you going to fuck around?"

A husband and wife are asleep. All of a sudden, the wife turns on the light, wakes up the husband, and says, "Honey, when I die, will you find a girlfriend and get married again?"

"No," says the husband, still half asleep. "I'll never get married after you've gone. I would never do that."

"It's O.K. if you do," says the wife. "I want you to be happy, and if you marry your girlfriend, it will make me happy, too."

He murmurs "O.K.," rolls over, and she turns off the light.

Two minutes later, the wife turns on the light and says, "Honey, when I die and you marry your girlfriend, will you live in this house?"

Still groggy, the husband says, "No, I won't live in this house, if I remarry."

"It's O.K. if you do," says the wife. "I know you love this house and I'll be happy if you live here with your new wife."

"O.K.," says the sleepy husband, "I'll stay in this house." He rolls over and falls back to sleep and the wife turns off the light.

Two minutes later the wife turns on the light again and says, "Honey, if you marry your girlfriend and stay in this house, will you sleep in this bed with your new wife?"

The husband says, "No, we won't sleep in this bed."

"It's O.K. if you do," says the wife. "I want you to be happy and I know you love this bed, it will make me happy if you do."

"O.K.," says the husband as he rolls over to get some sleep, "we'll sleep in this bed." The wife turns off the light.

One minute later, the wife turns the light back on and says, "Honey, when you marry your girl-friend and stay in this house and sleep in this bed, will you let your new wife use my golf clubs?"

"Hell, no," says the husband as he rolls over. "She's left-handed!"

A golfer can't see his golf balls. A soon as the ball is hit, the guy can't follow them and he loses eighteen balls per round. He asks the golf pro for help.

The golf pro says, "Take the club's ball watcher with you. He sees all the balls and where they go. He's right outside. Play nine and see for yourself."

The guy goes outside and sees an old man sitting in a chair, asleep. He goes back in the clubhouse and says, "I only see an old man, asleep, out there."

"That's him," says the pro. "Wake him up and take him with you." The guy goes out, gently wakes the old man up, and they both walk to the first tee.

The guy tees off and, as usual, he loses sight of the ball. "Did you see where it went?" he asks the ball watcher.

"Yeah," the ball watcher says. "I see it."

They get in the cart and drive to where the ball

headed. "Well, are you sure you saw it?" asks the guy, looking around for his ball.

"Yeah," says the old man. "I saw it."

"Well, where's my ball?" asks the guy.

"I can't remember," says the old man.

A guy with a speech impediment—he stutters—gets a job selling books door-to-door. On his first day, the sales manager gives him some books and sends him out and at five o'clock he returns with all receipts, no books.

The second day, the sales manager loads him up with more books than the first day and sends him out. He returns at five o'clock with all the receipts, no books.

The third day, the sales manager really loads him up with books, more than the first two days combined, and sends him out. At five o'clock he returns and gives the sales manager all of the receipts for all the books he had.

"This is truly amazing," says the sales manager. "In three days you have sold more books than my top salesman does in a week. What's your sales pitch?"

"W-w-well," says the salesman, "I s-s-say, 'D-d-do, y-y-you w-w-want t-t-to b-b-b-buy a b-b-b-book or d-do y-you w-want m-me t-to r-read it t-to y-you?'"

A skeleton walks into a bar, walks up to the bartender and says, "Give me a beer and a mop."

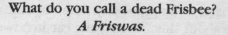

What do you call a dead Frisbee?
A Friswas.

Why do Scotsmen wear kilts?
*Because sheep run away at the sound
of zippers.*

Why do birds fly south for the winter?
It's too far to walk.

Why don't bunnies make noise
when they make love?
Because they have cotton balls.

It has been recently proven that carrots are good for the eyes. A major research project has shown that almost no rabbits wear glasses.

A man and a woman are having drinks when they get into a discussion about who enjoys sex more. The man says, "Men obviously enjoy sex more than women. Why do you think we're so obsessed with getting laid?"

"That doesn't prove anything," says the woman. "Think about this; when your ear itches and you put your little finger in it and wiggle it around, then pull it out, which feels better, your ear or your finger?"

And God created woman and she had three breasts. God then asked the woman, "Is there anything that you'd like to have changed?"

The woman replied, "Yes, could you get rid of this middle breast?" And so it was done and it was good.

Then the woman exclaimed as she held the third breast in her hand, "What can be done with this useless boob?"

And God created man.

How do we know that God is a man?
If God were a woman,
sperm would taste like chocolate.

When God was creating the human race, he lined up all the males on one side and all the females on the other side. Then he asked, "Which of your species would like to urinate standing up.

The males went crazy, shouting that they all wanted to pee standing up.

"Fine," said God. "Women get multiple orgasms."

Why do one out of five women go to heaven?
If all five went, it would be hell!

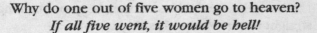

What did God say after creating man?
"I can do better."

Why are men smarter when making love?
They are plugged into a know-it-all.

The morning after their honeymoon night, the wife says to her husband, "You know, you are a lousy lover!"

The husband replies, "How would you know after only thirty seconds?"

A man parks his car at the supermarket and is walking past an empty cart when he hears a woman ask, "Excuse me, do you want that cart?"

"No," he answers, "I'm only after one thing."

As he walks toward the store, he hears her murmur under her breath, "Typical male!"

🍸

A guy in California buys a red, sleek, powerful Lamborghini. He decides to open it up on the long, straight desert road to Las Vegas.

On the way, he stops at a "last gas" gas station to fill it up. The attendant comes out, wearing greasy overalls, and it is obvious that he has never seen a car like the Lamborghini. The guy tells him to fill the tank while he goes to the bathroom.

As the guy comes out of the bathroom, he sees the attendant sitting in the front seat of his new car. He is furious and runs over, grabs the attendant by his greasy overalls, pulls him out, gets in, closes the door, and takes off.

As he is driving along at 80 mph, he looks in his rearview mirror and sees something coming up behind him, very fast. Determined not to let anyone outrun him, he speeds up to 100 mph.

He looks in the mirror, and whatever it is, is still behind him and moving fast. He speeds up to 150 mph, but the thing is still behind him. His curiosity gets the best of him and he slows down to 50 mph. All of a sudden, the thing flies past him at an incredible rate of speed, so fast that the guy still can't make out what it is. So he brings the Lamborghini back up to 150 mph.

He sees the object and thinks he is catching up—but he is not catching up at all. The thing is coming toward him and zips past going in the other direction. Now the guy is so confused that he stops his car.

All of a sudden he sees the thing from his rearview mirror come straight at him, and it slams in the back of the new Lamborghini. The guy gets out and sees the gas attendant from the station lying on the pavement behind the car.

"What the hell are you doing?" screams the guy.

The attendant looks up at the guy and says, weakly, "When you threw me out of your car, my suspenders got caught in the door!"

🍺

Two hobos run in to each other. "I haven't seen you in a while, where have you been?" asks the first hobo.

"Well," says the second hobo, "I was walking along the railroad tracks and I saw a woman tied to the tracks, so I untied her and had sex with her, fell asleep, woke up, and had sex again."

"Wow!" says the first hobo. "That sounds great. What does she look like?"

"I don't know," says the second hobo. "I couldn't find her head!"

A patient is talking to his psychiatrist. "I love boxer shorts," he says.

The shrink says, "Nothing wrong with that. I prefer them myself."

"Really?" says the patient. "With mustard or mayonnaise?"

A guy walks into a bar with an octopus. He says, "I'll bet fifty dollars that my octopus can play any musical instrument you give him."

Someone gives the octopus an old guitar. The octopus looks at the guitar, tunes the strings, and plays a beautiful Spanish flamenco tune. Fifty dollars to the guy with the octopus.

Another man hands the octopus a trumpet. The octopus looks it over, loosens up the valves, licks his lips, and plays a fantastic jazz solo. The guy pockets another fifty dollars.

The bartender walks to the storeroom and comes out with a set of bagpipes and puts it on the bar. "I'll give you a hundred dollars if the octopus can play this!" he says.

The octopus takes a long, hard look at the bagpipes, lifts it up, turns it over, has another look from a different angle, studying the bagpipes.

The guy says, "What are you waiting for? Play the damn thing!"

"Play it?" says the octopus. "Hell, if I can figure out how to get its pajamas off, I'm going to fuck it!"

A guy walks into a bar with a monkey. He orders a drink and the monkey starts wandering around and ends up on top of the pool table. The bartender watches as the monkey picks up the eight ball, puts it in his mouth, and swallows it.

The bartender is furious. "That eight ball is the owner's pride and joy! It's made of pure ivory and has been in his family for generations!" He kicks the guy and his monkey out of the bar.

Two weeks later, the guy and his monkey return to the bar and he gives the bartender the eight ball, all cleaned up, as good as new, and he apologizes.

As the guy is talking to the bartender, the monkey picks up a peanut from a bowl, shoves it up his ass, takes it out, and eats it. The bartender sees this and says to the guy, "*Now* what the hell is the monkey doing?"

"Oh," says the guy. "Ever since the eight ball, he just wants to make sure what he is eating!"

A pony walks into a bar and says, "How about a hot toddy? I'm a little hoarse."

An Irish guy walks into a bar and sits down, not saying a word. The bartender sees him and says, "Let me get you a drink."

The Irishman says, "I'll have an Irish whiskey, neat."

The bartender gives him his drink, and the Irish guy downs it and starts to leave. The bartender says, "Hey, you owe me for that drink!"

"Well, sir," says the Irish guy, "I don't believe I owe you anything. You offered it to me."

A lawyer sitting at the bar says to the bartender, "Technically, he is correct. He didn't ask for anything. You offered him the drink."

The bartender is so pissed off that he picks up the Irish guy and throws him out of the bar.

Three days later, the Irish guy walks back into the same bar and sits down. The bartender says, "Didn't I throw you out of here a few days ago?"

"No, I don't believe you did," says the Irish guy.

"You sure do look like the guy I threw out," says the bartender.

"No, I'm not the guy," says the Irish guy.

"Well," says the bartender, "you must have a double!"

The Irish guy says, "Thank you, make it an Irish whiskey."

Where does an Irish family go on vacation?
A different bar.

A blonde is walking past a construction site and sees a help-wanted sign. She walks up to the foreman and says, "I want to apply for the job."

The foreman says, "Well, I need someone with experience."

The blonde says, "I have fifteen years of construction experience."

The foreman says, "I need someone right now, so I'll give you a shot. You'll be working on the ninth floor. If I need anything, I'll signal you. You know all the hand signals?"

"Yes," says the blonde.

"Good," says the foreman. "Go up to the ninth floor. The blueprints and tools are up there."

After a few hours, the foreman whistles and the blonde looks down. With hand signals, the foreman points to his eye, then his knee, and then makes a sawing motion with his arm. The blonde responds by pointing to her eye, touching her left breast, and grabbing her crotch.

The foreman shakes his head and goes to the ninth floor. "I thought you said you knew the hand signals," he says. "What I was saying was, I 'eye,' need, 'knee,' a saw—that was when I moved my arm back and forth. I need a saw!"

The blonde says, "I know. What I said when I pointed to my eye, then touched my left breast, then grabbed my crotch, was, 'I left it in the box'!"

What's the difference between a blonde
and a brick?
*When you lay a brick, it doesn't follow you
around for two weeks whining.*

What's the difference between medium
and rare?
Six inches is medium, eight inches is rare.

Why do elephants have four feet?
Eight inches just ain't enough.

Why don't men fake orgasms?
*Because no man would make those faces
on purpose!*

What do toilets, a clitoris, and an
anniversary have in common?
Men miss them all.

Did you hear about the new blonde paint?
*It's not real bright, but it's cheap
and spreads easy.*

Ask your friend this:

Which sexual position produces the ugliest children?
Ask your mother!

Four Irish brothers come to New York and get
jobs as cab drivers. Because they come from a
small village in Ireland, they can't get the grasp of
stoplights and they all run the red lights. One of
the brothers is driving a guy downtown when all
of a sudden he stops at a green light.

"Hey," says the guy, "why did you stop at a green light?"

The Irishman replies, "One of my brothers might be coming!"

Υ

There is a massive traffic jam in Times Square. A cop shows up and sees a penguin in the middle of Broadway. He picks it up, opens the door of the first car he sees, throws the penguin in and says, "Do me a favor, take this penguin to the zoo."

The guy takes a right and heads to the Bronx.

Four hours later the guy, with the penguin still sitting in the front seat, is at a light on 42nd Street. The same cop is on the corner and sees him. He walks over to the car and says, "I thought I told you to take the penguin to the zoo."

"I did," says the guy. "Now we are going to dinner and then the opera!"

Υ

A Polish guy is not doing too good at the entrance exam for the police department. The sergeant, who is also Polish, feels sorry for him and wants to help him pass the test. "I'll tell you what," he says, "I'll give you one last question. Go home, research it, and bring me the answer the first thing in the morning. The question is, Who killed Jesus Christ?"

The Pole goes home and his wife says, "How did the exam go?"

"Great!" says the Pole. "I'm working on my first murder case!"

Do you know what happened to the
Polish rocket ship?
At five hundred feet it ran out of coal!

How do you confuse a Polish guy?
*Put him in a round room and tell him
to piss in the corner.*

Can't just pick on the Polish, now, can we?

How do Greeks separate the men from the boys?
With a crowbar.

Why do Greek men wear gold chains
around their necks?
So they know where to stop shaving.

As I was leaving my apartment to go to work, I noticed the police were at the apartment down the hall. I walked over to a cop and asked, "What's going on?"

"There has been a murder," the cop says.

"How did it happen?" I ask.

"The victim," says the cop, "was found in the bathtub filled with milk and cornflakes."

Right away, I knew it was the work of a cereal killer!

A guy goes to his doctor and says, "Doc, I have a problem."

The doctor asks, "What kind of problem?"

The guy says, "Well, before I go to work, my wife jumps me and we have sex three times. When I get to work, my secretary and I have sex, then at lunch we have sex and a 'quickie' at the end of work. Then when I get home, my wife jumps me again and we have sex before dinner, after dinner, before we go to bed, and before we go to sleep. All this happens every day."

"So," asks the doctor, "what's your problem?"

The guy says, "When I jerk off, I get dizzy."

A guy calls 911. "Help, send an ambulance! My wife is in labor and her water broke!"

The 911 operator asks, "Is this her first child?"

"No, you moron!" yells the guy. "This is her husband!"

🍸

Two teenagers are on their first date and they go to the amusement park. After going on the roller coaster and the Ferris wheel, the boy asks his date, "What do you want to do now?"

"I want to get weighed," she responds.

They head off to the guy that guesses your weight. The kid pays the guy, he guesses her weight, and then they go to the bumper cars, then to the funhouse. "What do you want to do now?" asks the kid again.

"I want to get weighed!" urges his date.

So they go back to the guy that guesses your weight, the kid pays him and he guesses both their weights, they go back to the roller coaster, eat some cotton candy and hot dogs, then he takes her home. When the girl walks in her house, her mother asks, "How was your date?"

"Wowsy!" she replies.

🍺

Why is college like a woman?
It takes forever to get in and nine months later you wish you hadn't come.

🍸

What has a whole bunch of balls and
scrolls old ladies?
A bingo machine.

What three two-letter words mean "small"?
"Is it in?"

This is for you computer geeks:

A girl said, "Give a gig, and make it hurt!"
So I gave three 340MB and slapped her with a
SCSI adapter.

I went to the county fair and they had one of
those "Believe it or Not" shows. They had a man
born with a penis *and* a brain!

How did the blonde try to kill a pigeon?
She threw it off the Empire State Building.

What do you have when you have
two balls in your hand?
A man's undivided attention.

A young Jewish boy is very incorrigible. He won't clean his room, he won't do his chores, and he has been thrown out of every school in town. Finally, his desperate parents send him to a Catholic school. Almost immediately, his room is clean, all his chores are done, and he is getting straight A's in school.

His father says, "So, what was it that made you change your ways?"

The kid says, "The nuns gave me a tour of the school and showed me where everything is, and I met the Monsignor, who took me to the chapel and showed me what happened to the last Jewish boy who got out of line!"

An architectural engineer dies and goes to heaven. St. Peter is at the Gates and asks for his occupation, and the guy tells him. St. Peter looks at the book and can't find him. He punches in the information in the Cray computer—still no architectural engineer.

St. Peter says, "We're not supposed to have an architectural engineer for another ten years. You probably took a wrong turn somewhere and belong in hell."

The engineer says, "Look, I'm a God-fearing man. I never did anything wrong my whole life. I belong here!"

St. Peter takes him by the arm, walks him to an elevator, and says, "Push the double L button and you'll be there in no time."

The next thing the guy knows, he's in hell. Satan greets him and asks, "What's your occupation?"

"Architectural engineer," the guy says.

"Man," says Satan, "Do I need you! Look at this place. It's hot, there's fire everywhere, and my throne is a mess! I'll make it worth your while if you can do something about this."

A month later, God calls Satan, "Satan, how ya doing? Look, there was a glitch in the computer and the architectural engineer you have belongs up here. Send him back up, will you?"

"No way!" Satan says. "You should see what that guy has done to this place! The fire is directed through beautiful glass tubes, we have central air-conditioning, and my throne is a masterpiece! And there's a bunch of other stuff he needs to do for me, so there is no way I'm sending him back to you!"

"Satan," God says menacingly, "send him back or I'll sue you for every penny you've got! You won't have a throne to sit on!"

"Oh, yeah?" says Satan. "Where are you going to get a lawyer?"

What's the difference between
a proud chicken and a lawyer?
One clucks defiant.

Did you hear about the blind skunk?
He fucked a piece of shit.

Did you hear about the truck carrying
copies of Roget's Thesaurus that overturned
on the highway?
*The local newspaper reported that the
onlookers were "stunned, overwhelmed,
astonished, bewildered, and dumbfounded."*

*I always thought that a thesaurus was a
smart dinosaur!*

Did you hear about the red ship and
the blue ship that collided?
The survivors were marooned.

A friend of mine asked me what I thought of
Flushing, New York. I said it was a great idea.

If FedEx and UPS merged, would they call it
Fed UP?

How many men does it take to tile a bathroom?
Two, if you slice them very thinly.

A wife wants bigger breasts. She says to her husband, "Honey, I've tried everything except implants and I'm not going to go through that."

Her husband says, "Why don't you try rubbing toilet paper between your breasts?"

"Do you think that will work?" asks the wife.

"Why not?" says her husband. "It worked pretty good on your ass."

A guy meets a woman on the golf course. They agree to play golf together the next day. They play and find that they have a lot in common, so they decide to play golf together for the rest of the week. On the last day of golf they go out to dinner, have a wonderful meal and stimulating conversation. Out in the parking lot of the restaurant, they kiss passionately.

The guy says softly, "I want to make love to you, I want to be inside you!".

The woman says, "I have to tell you, I'm a transvestite."

"You bitch!" yells the guy angrily. "You've been playing off the red tees!"

What's an Australian kiss?
The same as a French kiss,
only down under.

What do you see when you look in
a blonde's eyes?
The back of her head.

What are the two reasons why men
don't mind their own business?
No mind. No business.

What do blondes and beer bottles
have in common?
They are both empty from the neck up.

Did you hear about the Polish guy who won
a gold medal at the Olympics?
He was so proud, he had it bronzed.

What's one sign that you drank too much?
You wake up in Montana with a Mohawk.
Not the haircut—a big sweaty Indian!

And remember, it's: One tequila, two tequila, three tequila, floor!

Cecil B. de Mille, perhaps one of the greatest filmmakers of all time, was directing his latest movie. He had to shoot a difficult battle scene, using thousands of extras as gladiators fighting in a huge outdoor stadium. C.B., as he was known on the movie set, strategically placed seventeen cameras all around the stadium to capture every movement of the extras. It was very important that the whole scene be shot in one take, by all seventeen cameras, or the scene would be ruined, so he gave each of the seventeen cameramen walkie-talkies so he could coordinate the shots.

Finally, Cecil B. de Mille was ready to shoot the scene. Perched on his boom camera, he radioed camera number one. "Camera one," said C.B., "are you ready?"

"Ready when you are, C.B.!" replied camera one.

"Camera two," said C.B., "are you ready?"

"Ready when you are, C.B.!" replied camera two.

He did the same for the rest of the camera operators and all the cameramen responded with, "Ready when you are, C.B.!"

"Roll cameras and action!" yelled de Mille into his walkie-talkie, and the thousands of extras went into action while the cameras rolled.

After ten long minutes, de Mille yelled, "Cut! Camera one, did you get it?"

"Got it, C.B.!" said camera one.

"Camera two, did you get it?" asked C.B.

"Got it, C.B.!" said camera two.

He asked the same question for all the cameras up to number sixteen and they all responded with, "Got it, C.B.!"

Finally he asked camera seventeen, "Camera seventeen, did you get it?"

"Ready when you are, C.B.!" came the voice over the walkie-talkie.

🍸

And speaking of movies . . . I promised this joke to my parents.

On the set of Ginger Rogers's last movie. The stage is set, the cameras are ready, and the director tells the assistant director to go get Miss Rogers from her dressing room. The A.D. knocks on her door, but there is no answer. He tells the director that he can't find her anywhere.

The director then tells everyone to go look for

her. People are searching high and low. Finally, a stagehand runs up to the director and says, "I found her! I found her!"

"Where was she?" asks the director.

The stagehand replies, "I found her under Astaire!"

🍺

Two Polish guys are drinking in a bar. The first Polish guy says to the other, "Hey, how was your honeymoon?"

The second Polish guy says, "It was great, and you know, the way she was acting, I think I could have gotten laid!"

🍸

What do a tornado and marriage have in common?
In the beginning, there's a lot of sucking and blowing, then you lose your house!

🍺

A guy walks into a barber shop and asks the barber, "How long is the wait?"

The barber says, "About two hours." The guy leaves.

The next day, the guy walks into the barber shop and asks, "How long is the wait?"

The barber says, "About an hour and a half." The guy leaves.

The next day, the guy walks in again and asks, "How long is the wait?"

"About forty-five minutes," says the barber, and the guy leaves.

Curious, the barber says to a customer, "Do me a favor, follow that guy and tell me where he goes. He's been coming in all week asking me how long the wait is. I have the only shop in town and I've never given him a haircut."

An hour later, the customer comes back and says, "I found out where that guy goes."

"Oh, and where's that?" asks the barber.

"Your house," says the customer.

🍸

Three guys are in line at the Pearly Gates. St. Peter asks the first guy, "What's your story, how did you die?"

The first guy says, "I came home early, saw my wife naked, and I noticed a cigar in the ashtray. I don't smoke cigars, so I looked out the window and I saw a guy run out of my apartment building to the street, frantically hailing a cab. I snapped, picked up the refrigerator, and threw it out the window. The strain was too much for me and I had a heart attack."

St. Peter asks the second guy, "How about you, how did you die?"

"Well," says the second guy, "I was late for work one day and I was running out of my building trying to get a cab when a refrigerator fell on me."

St. Peter asks the third guy, "And you, how did you die?"

The third guy says, "I was hiding in this refrigerator ..."

Do infants enjoy infancy the way adults enjoy adultery?

Two guys are sitting on a park bench on a cold, damp day. A beautiful woman walks by and one guy says, "Tickle your ass with a feather?"

"What?" asks the woman.

"I said," says the guy, "particularly nasty weather."

The woman smiles, and the guy gets up and walks away with her.

The other guy thought that was a great pickup line and decides to use it. When another beautiful woman walks by, he says, "Stick a feather up your ass?"

The woman says, "Excuse me?"

"Fucking cold, isn't it?" says the guy.

What's the difference between mad cow disease and a woman with PMS?
NOTHING!!!!!!!

This one is courtesy of my son, Michael!

A traveling salesman's car breaks down near a farmhouse. He knocks on the door and the farmer says, "Yes?"

The salesman says, "My car broke down, can I spend the night?"

The farmer says, "Sure, but you'll have to sleep with my son."

"Your son?" says the salesman. "Wait a minute, I must be in the wrong joke!"

🍸

What's the name of the guy from India
who works the coat room at the Plaza?
Mahatma Coat.

🍸

Did you hear about the gay midget?
He came out of the cupboard.

🍸

Did you hear about the Mexican who tried
to commit suicide?
*He tried to hang himself from the
rearview mirror.*

🍸

What's smaller than a teeny, weeny fly?
A fly's teeny weeny.

A woman goes to a gynecologist for the first time. She is on the examining table with her feet in the stirrups and the gynecologist says, "Now, we're going to start with some numbness."

The woman, confused, says, "What do you mean?"

The gynecologist leans in real close between her legs and mumbles, "Num-num-num-num-num ...

A guy goes to a pharmacy, walks up to the pharmacist and says, "I need some birth control pills for my fourteen-year-old daughter."

"You mean to tell me," says the pharmacist, "that your fourteen-year-old daughter is sexually active?"

"Hell, no," says the guy. "She just lies there and doesn't move like her mother!"

Did you know that there are over fifty thousand battered women in the United States? And all this time I've been eating them plain!

A guy goes to a church and walks into the confessional. "Forgive me, Father, for I have sinned," he says.

The priest says, "What is it that brings you here?"

"Well, Father," says the guy, "I used the F-word over the weekend."

"How did this come about?" asks the priest.

"Well, Father," says the guy, "I was playing golf and on the first tee I hit a slice into the trees."

"And that's when you cursed out loud?" asks the priest.

"Oh no, not yet," says the guy. "Well, I got lucky. I found my ball and had a clear shot to the green when, all of a sudden, a squirrel came out of the bushes, picked up my ball by its teeth, and scampered up a tree."

"That must have been when you cursed," says the priest.

"No," says the guy, "because just as the squirrel got to the top of the tree, a hawk swooped down and grabbed it with its talons. The hawk flew out over the green and the squirrel dropped the ball, which landed five inches from the cup."

"Oh, I see, that's when you cursed," the priest says assuredly.

"No, not then, you see—"

The priest interrupts, "Don't tell me you missed the fucking putt!"

🍸

A man goes to confession. "Forgive me, Father, for I have sinned," he says. "I haven't been to confession in a long time and I have a sin that has been weighing heavily on mine and my family's conscience for many years."

"What is your sin, my son?" asks the priest.

"We hid a family of Jews from the Nazis," says the man.

"My son," says the priest, "saving a family from certain death is not a sin."

"We charged them five hundred dollars a month," says the man.

"Well," says the priest, "was it agreeable to them? Did the expense cause them any hardship?"

"Oh yes, they agreed, Father, and they could afford the money," says the man.

"Did they have enough food and were they healthy?" asks the priest.

"Yes, Father, they had plenty of food, they were healthy," says the man.

The priest thinks for a moment and says, "My son, you and your family haven't committed any sin. I don't know what you are worried about."

"But Father," says the man, "should I tell them that the war is over?"

Hear about the cross-eyed teacher who couldn't control her pupils?

A Texas rancher and a New Hampshire farmer are talking. "How big is your farm?" asks the Texas rancher.

"Well, my farm is a little over two hundred acres," says the New Hampshire farmer.

"Son," bellows the Texas rancher, "my ranch is so big, I can get in my truck on one end and it will take me three days to reach the other end!"

"Uh-huh," says the New Hampshire farmer. "I had a truck like that once."

What's the real state motto of Texas?
Don't mess with Texas, we're armed!

What's the real state motto of
New Hampshire?
Leave us the fuck alone!

If Bo Derek married Don Ho, she'd be Bo Ho.

If Bea Arthur married Sting, she'd be Bea Sting.

If Dolly Parton married Salvador Dali, she'd
be Dolly Dali.

If G. Gordon Liddy married Boutrous Boutrous-
Ghali, then divorced him to marry Kenny G., he'd
be G. Ghali G.

This one's for all you baseball fans ...

If Boog Powell married Felipe Alou, he'd be
Boog Alou.

What's the difference between a Porsche
and a soprano?
*Not too many musicians have been
in a Porsche.*

A man is complaining to a friend: "I had it all—
money, a beautiful house, a nice car, a great motorcycle, the love of a beautiful woman. Then it was
all gone!"

"What happened?" asks the friend.

"My wife found out!" says the man.

How many chiropractors does it take
to screw in a lightbulb?
One, but you have to make five visits.

Scientists revealed that beer contains small
traces of female hormones. To prove their theory,
they fed 100 men 12 pints of beer and observed
that 100 percent of them gained weight, talked
incessantly without making sense, and couldn't
drive.

No further testing is planned.

Two Italians, Pietro and Marchello, are talking. Pietro says to Marchello, "Marchello, do you like women with tiny mustaches and moles on their cheeks with hair coming out?"

Marchello says, "No, Pietro, I don't like women like that."

"Marchello," says Pietro, "do you like women with hairy underarms and hairy legs?"

"No, Pietro," says Marchello, "I don't like women like that at all!"

"Marchello," says Pietro, "do you like women with saggy tits and fat asses?"

"No, Pietro," says Marchello, "I don't like women like that!"

"Then Marchello," says Pietro, "why are you fucking my wife?"

Two Russians are standing in a very long line waiting to buy some vodka. The line is so long that one Russian says to the other, "I can't stand this anymore! Always waiting in line to buy anything! I'm going to shoot the Minister of Commerce!" He leaves the line and storms out.

Hours later, the other Russian finally buys his vodka and starts to walk out. As he is walking past the very long line, he sees his friend standing at the end of the line. "Hey," he says to his friend, "I thought you were going to shoot the Commerce Minister."

"I was," says his friend, "but the line is too long!"

The phone rings in Saddam Hussein's office. "Hello?" says Saddam.

"Hello, Saddam?" says the caller. "This is Paddy up in County Cork, Ireland. I'm ringing to inform you that we are officially declaring war on you!"

"Well, Paddy," says Saddam, "how big is your army?"

"At this moment in time," says Paddy, "there is myself, my cousin Sean, my next-door neighbor Gerry, and the entire dart team from the pub. That makes eight!"

"I must tell you Paddy," says Saddam, "I have one million men in my army waiting to move on my command."

"Begorra!" says Paddy, "I'll have to ring you back!"

The next day, Paddy calls Hussein. "Saddam, the war is still on! We have managed to acquire some equipment!"

"What equipment would that be, Paddy?" asks Saddam.

"Well, we have two International Harvester combines, a bulldozer, and Murphy's tractor from the farm!" says Paddy.

"I must tell you, Paddy," says Saddam, "that I have 16,000 tanks, 14,000 armored personnel carriers, and my army has increased to one and a half million since we last spoke."

"Really?" says Paddy. "I'll have to ring you back!"

The next day, Paddy calls Hussein. "Saddam," says Paddy, "the war is still on! We have managed to get ourselves airborne! We've modified Ted's ultralight with a couple of rifles in the cockpit, and the dominoes team has joined us as well!"

"I must tell you, Paddy," says Saddam, "that I have 1,000 bombers, 500 MiG-19 attack jets, my military complex is surrounded by laser-guided surface-to-air missile sites, and since we last spoke, my army has increased to two million."

"Jesus, Mary, and Joseph!" says Paddy. "I'll have to ring you back!"

Paddy calls again the next day. "Mr. Hussein," he says, "I am sorry to tell you that we have to call off the war."

Saddam Hussein says, "It is I who am sorry that you called off the war. But tell me, Paddy, why are you calling it off?"

"Well," says Paddy, "we've had a chat and there's no way we can feed two million prisoners!"

🍺

Margaret is concerned that Paddy drinks too much. She decides the only way to stop him from drinking is to scare the shit out of him. One night while Paddy is at the pub, Margaret rummages through the closet and finds an old Halloween costume of the devil. She puts on the cap and the mask with the horns and goes out to the graveyard that separates their house and the pub and hides behind a gravestone to wait for Paddy.

Sure enough, like clockwork, Paddy stumbles out of the pub as it closes and takes the path through the graveyard to his house. Halfway down the path, Margaret jumps out from behind a gravestone, dressed in the devil's costume, and says menacingly, "I'M THE DEVIL!"

Without batting an eyelash, Paddy says, "Well, it's nice to meet you. You know I married your sister?"

You know you're too drunk when the back of your head keeps getting hit by the toilet seat.

Well, here it is, the very first long joke I ever told.

A Kentucky colonel and the devil had an argument. The devil said that no one had a perfect memory, while the colonel claimed that there was an Indian on his plantation who never forgot anything. The colonel agreed to give up his soul to the devil if the Indian ever did forget anything.

They went out to a part of the plantation to meet the Indian. The devil went up to him and said, "Do you like eggs?"

The Indian replied, "Yes." The devil then went away.

Twenty years later the colonel died. "Here's my chance to get his soul!" thought the devil. He went back to the plantation and found the Indian. Raising his hand, he gave the tribal greeting, "How."

Quick as a wink, the Indian replied, "Fried."

Well, I hope you had as much fun reading this book as I had putting it together. It's amazing what one can accomplish with a couple of cases of beer in you!

Thank you and good night!

About the Author

JIMMY PRITCHARD was born in Texas, raised in Massachusetts, and he lived in New Hampshire for ten years before coming to New York City. As an actor he has been in numerous stage productions, radio voice-overs, and a commercial. He was also a member of the sketch comedy group Chubby Runs Away. An avid skier, he also enjoys scuba diving and is desperately trying to break one hundred on his golf game. He especially loves tooling around on his motorcycle, a 1978 750cc Yamaha Special (with a drive shaft). He and his wife, Lisa, split their time between the country in Massachusetts and the City of New York.